The Strange Wondrous Works of Eleanor Eleanor

The Fence Modern Poets Series

The Strange Wondrous Works of
ELEANOR ELEANOR

A CATALOG

with an Introduction by KATHRYN COWLES

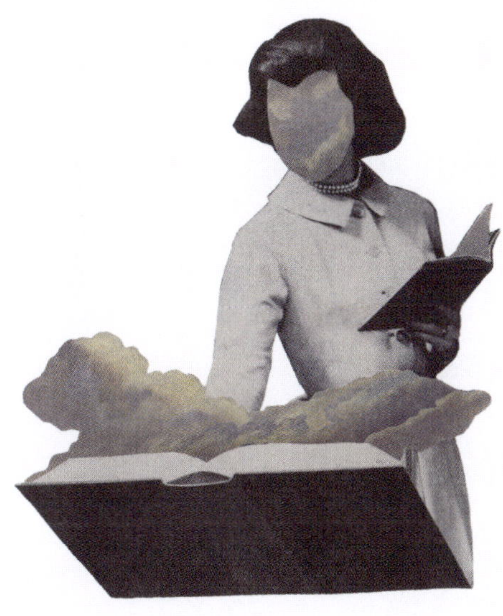

Fence Books   Astoria, New York   2025

FENCE BOOKS

The Strange Wondrous Works of Eleanor Eleanor, 2025
Copyright © 2025 Kathryn Cowles
Collage images © 2025 Kathryn Cowles
Cover image "From Above Wing Lady" by Kathryn Cowles

THE FENCE MODERN POETS SERIES PRIZE
Emily Wallis Hughes, Editor
Published in the United States by Fence Books
36-09 28th Avenue, Apartment 3R
Astoria, NY 11103-4518
www.fenceportal.org

This book was printed at Versa Press
Fence Books are distributed by Consortium Book Sales and Distribution
Book design by Sharon DeGraw

The Fence Modern Poets Series is generously funded in part by the T.S. Eliot Foundation.

T. S. ELIOT FOUNDATION
Library of Congress Control Number: 2025948145
ISBN 13: 9798989978533

First Edition
First Printing
10 9 8 7 6 5 4 3 2

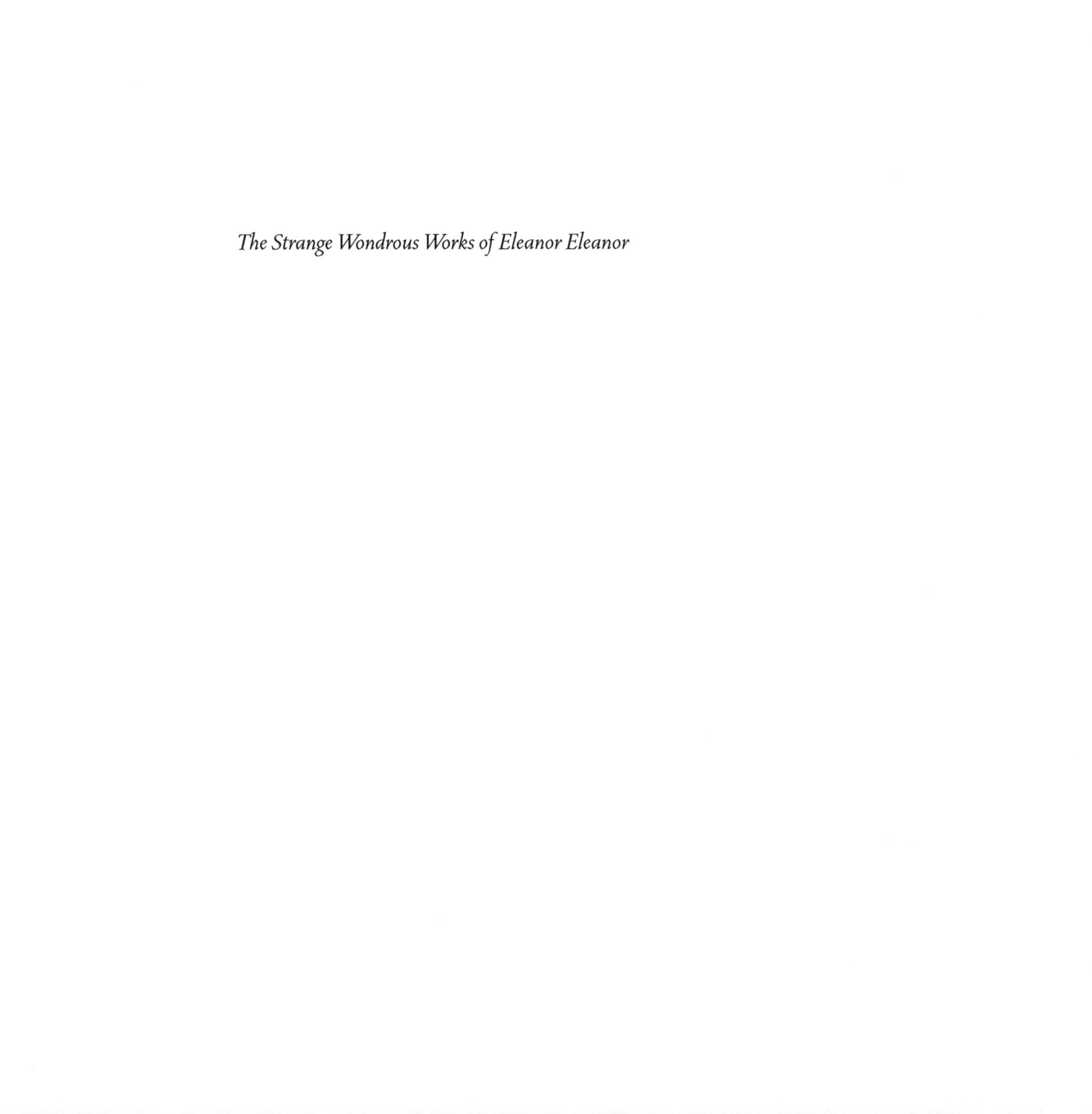

The Strange Wondrous Works of Eleanor Eleanor

Eleanor Eleanor and I were born in the same place in the same month in the same year, and though we veered apart now and then (she liked to wander, to live in the back of a bad car, to waitress somewhere for a month or work a season on a farm), we always found our way back into each other's company before long. But it has been more than a year now, and it's never been a year. She's just gone. And where? Everyone always wants to know.

Some think she started out on one of her famous long walks, only this particular day, she didn't walk back. Some think she and whatever she'd been working on drove themselves over a cliff, Ford Thunderbird suspended in air. If there is a witness protection program for reticent artists, maybe a witness protection program. After all, her daughter disappeared too. There's as good a chance as any that she sprouted actual wings, and as much evidence, so that's what I choose to believe.

When Eleanor Eleanor disappeared, at least half of the art she had made instantly disappeared, almost as if suddenly having never existed at all, evidenceless. When a tree falls in a forest, et cetera. When you are your own museum head and go off, so does the historical record. Some artists are compelled toward self-preservation, all acid-free and vacuum-sealed, climate-controlled and HD-scanned, archiving every last snip. Some artists are excellent executors of their own fiction. Like so many women before her, Eleanor Eleanor was not. But she did write things down. She sometimes said that her art works did not feel actually finished when she finished them. Perhaps she used the writing as addendum, as Derridian supplement. Because her art was so often experiential, conceptual, fleeting, fragile, or intentionally self-destroying, much of what we have left is this residual after-writing, a kind of fossil record that resists its own chronology.

This partial catalog, then, is an anti-chronological selection of her writings, which I found loosely shuffled on her otherwise cleared-off desk—a desk I never saw previously cleared in all the years I have known her, which is to say pretty much always. Seemed like a sign. On top was an otherwise blank notecard with my name on it.

After a year of being gone, Eleanor Eleanor has the indeterminacy of a metaphor for which we have only one side. Still, you can see it sometimes between the slats—her life. I have tried here to give form to something that will always be beyond form, to reanimate the left-behind, or perhaps to build a place, as Eleanor sometimes did, for ghosts to climb into. I hope, at the very least, to poke a peephole through which you can see a flash of movement, of her still-alive-ness, of feathers loosed.

—Kathryn Cowles, Editor, December 2025

Contents

Pregnant Belly

Pregnant Belly
Eleanor Eleanor (1979–)
Encaustic and pencil on paper
2020

In my pregnant belly was a map of Antarctica. Was an arctic fox was a white squirrel was a heart of scratched glass. You could only see the outlines. My pregnant belly was always under snow.

I perched atop my pregnant belly like a woman with a child with a bird in its hand. I was precarious. I was topheavy. My pregnant belly had its own heartbeat. My pregnant belly had its own furs, was under cover.

Even straight hallways were hard to maneuver. I grew every which way. My pregnant belly had its own elbows. My pregnant belly dropped. Sometimes the snow was really fruit tree blossoms. My pregnant belly cast alarming shadows and had its own grand piano.

My pregnant belly had a mind of its own. It longed to visit Antarctica. It kept me away from the ones I loved. My pregnant belly was visible through thicket. I liked to spy on my pregnant belly when it thought it went unobserved.

In my pregnant belly was a sea beast, was a sea was a sun was an underwater grotto. I perched atop my pregnant belly like a woman with a child with a bird in its hand. The bird tried to fly, but the child held tight. I groaned and groaned. I gave way to a hall. Snow fell, my pregnant belly fell, hand and foot. My legs bent every which way. My pregnant belly opened into Antarctica, into scratched glass. It was blossoms. It was ice.

Baby Ball
Eleanor Eleanor (1979–)
Magazine clippings, poem
2012

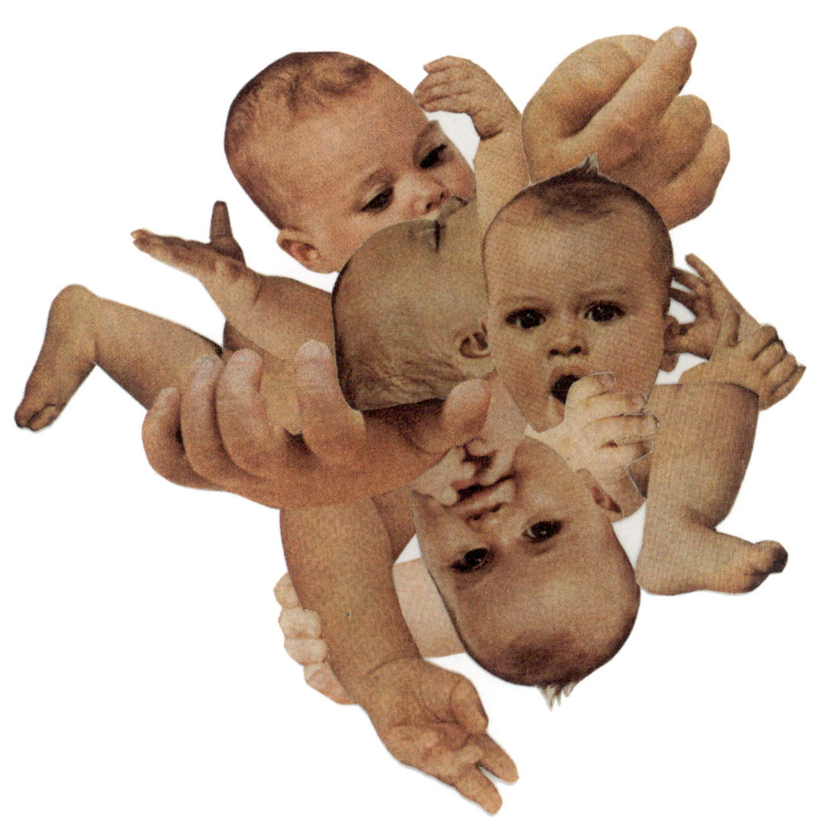

I feel an internal hinge. A popcorn kernel, a wing flap, feel
a breeze though no air, a leaf bud unraveled, a little latch.
I open my little out. I split
cells and cells again, and they
split off I am
a baby builder, I am
a copy machine, can make
with my eyes closed,
with both hands tied.

Nest 1
Eleanor Eleanor (1979 –)
Wood, egg tempera, lacquer
2012

The idea is Russian nesting dolls
only pregnant, great pregnant bellies
locking into one another
a great split at the waistline of each
a great opening out.
Let's say the outermost doll is a polygamist wife
because looking at a polygamist wife
is like looking forward and backward at once
like standing between two mirrors.
The polygamist wife suggests a line
of infinitely pregnant women
spanning in multiple directions around her.
The polygamist wife is a great great great great
grandmother of mine. And inside her shell
another pregnant woman. Inside her another and
another and my grandmother and my mother
with her hard-faced kind of love and
inside her is a doll of me, pregnant belly locked
in place. Split in advance, halved, thinly wooden
and covered with egg tempera and thick lacquer.
And inside my belly is a baby.

Moon
Eleanor Eleanor (1979 –   )
Oil on canvas
2020

This painting has no moon to see in it.
This painting has no flecks of snow,
no visible stars, no white point.
The reflection of the moon
has been unlaced from the lake in this painting
and so this painting has no lake to see.
The visible night lake
was always part moon
and there's no moon.
What of moon there is in this painting
one has to see some other way.
What of moon there is can be sensed
the way tiny nightblooming flowers
can be sensed beyond the door just
before you step into their wall of smell.
You can feel the edge of the smell,
the green fists of bud uncapping their whole
perfume bottles full of flake white paint
into the heavy air, a liquid mixed with another liquid.
What of moon there is
my baby has in her mouth as she latches me,
a hidden white in circulation
as, suck, suck, swallow,
she processes her bank transaction.
O blue bowl of white rice, I sense your individual grains

O moon making shadows but still hidden
behind the house
O salt I toss over my shoulder and feel fall
behind me, O wedding veil of salt,
you moon, you threshold, you unpack the lake
you bloom onto the face of my baby,
and this painting has a baby in it, a baby
and a lake behind her you cannot see.

I wrap my miniature, miscarried baby
in fine white linen then
fine softest red wool, which I wrap
in a miniature box of thin wood, the kind
with a one-way track and an invisible catch
that slides into place then snaps shut
forever and forever. And I wrap the box
in packing paper and twine
like a gift. I suspend
the miniature package with red silk thread
over my side of the bed
so my miniature, miscarried baby
and everything I've wrapped around her
can haunt me properly. Then I cut
the whole bed, chest of drawers,
wingback rocker, mirror, painting on the wall,
and the walls themselves,
the whole room, out of my house
and put it up in a room in a museum
where I go to sleep at night
leaving traces of myself on the things in the room
(hair on the pillows, new dust made out of my skin)
and alchemizing my small suspended package
into something new,
something entirely, entirely
other than what it was.

Heart 3
Eleanor Eleanor (1979–)
Thread, yarn, fabric, ribbon
2023

I start in the middle of a blank room and I take red thread, fine red thread made from linen or silk, and I stitch a rough heart shape into my skin over where my actual heart is, heart shaped like the organ rather than the cultural representation of a heart, I stitch and double stitch so the outline is thick and wooly (I have switched to wool thread—yarn, almost) then I darn the hollow space inside the outlines, I color it in with red, I stitch and cross over again with stitches, I embroider, I incorporate pieces of red fabric from items I have in my house, a plaid woolen blanket with tassels, just a little nip of fabric, hardly missed, a ribbon with shine on one side, flannel from the hem of my daughter's red nightgown, all this I stitch into the now quite large heart over my heart, concentric circles spreading like a sweater rash, a deep red I stitch together in layers, loose except where they latch on, radiating, hiding the layers that came before, pointing at the layers that came before, pointing with lights flashing.

Nest 2-4
Eleanor Eleanor (1979–)
Hair, hairspray, hairpins
2020–2021
       for Cami Nelson

My friend is a competitive hair artist.
She shapes atop the heads
of beautiful women
scenes from underwater grottos,
African plains. She is the best in the world.
I ask her first to make my hair
into a basket in which I can carry
my baby daughter and keep her close.
I have heard all daughters
turn from their mothers
one way or another so
when they told me I was pregnant
with a little girl that's when
I started to plan.
The basket takes several hours
of hairspray and pins.
Then I hold my baby on my head the way
women hold jugs of water
in some places where water is scarce.
After a month, my daughter's
motor skills have improved to where
she can shake loose from the basket so
she shakes loose from the basket.
I ask my friend to refashion it into

a cage, not to hold my daughter
but to hold a small animal
with which to lure my daughter to me.
A little yellow bird.
And I kneel on the ground so my daughter
can touch her fingers to the bars,
can sprinkle bird seed in and watch it eat.
My daughter outgrows the bird
or maybe it dies, no matter,
I get a tarantula
that eats live crickets,
which my daughter watches, enrapt,
but I know this cannot last forever
so I ask my friend to braid
my hair into that of my daughter
attached at the head,
the color identical, no way to tell
where one head ends and the other begins.

Things Look Different 1
Eleanor Eleanor (1979–)
Magazine clippings, tracing paper, type
2013

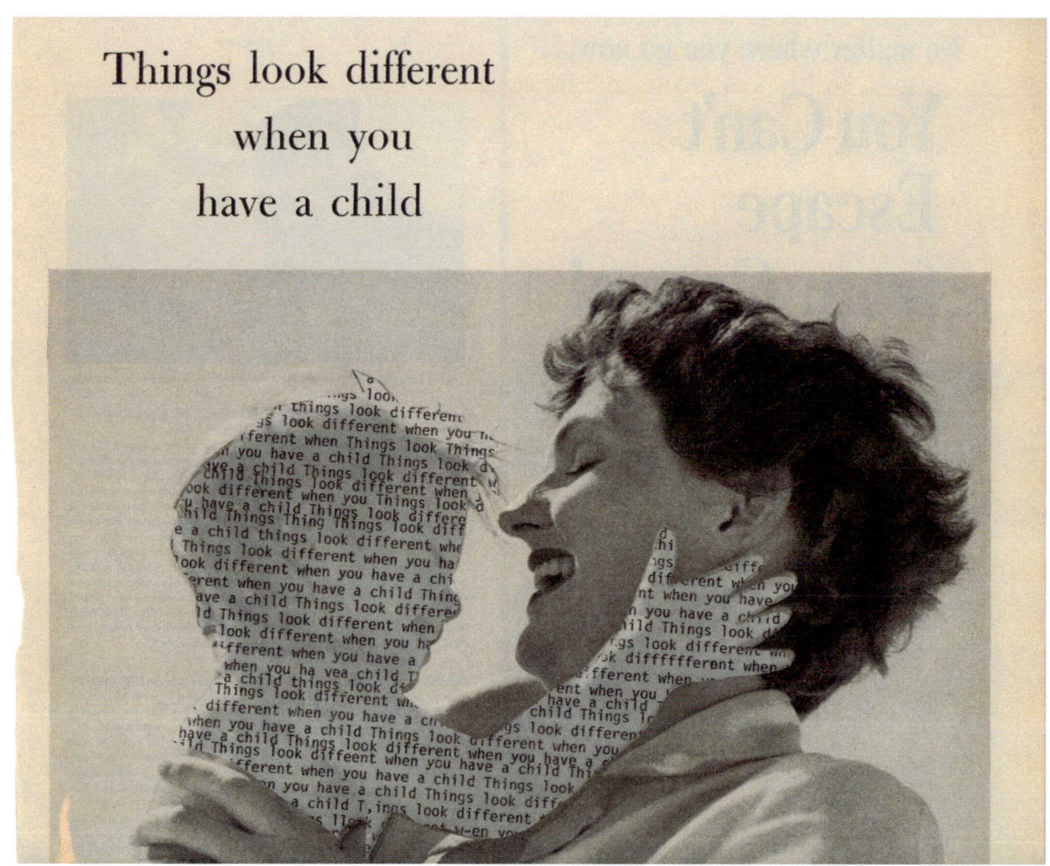

Things Look Different 2
Eleanor Eleanor (1979–)
Tracing paper, type

2013

Things look different when you have a child Things look different when you have a child things
look different when you have a child Things look different when you have a child Things look di
when you have a child things look different when you have a child Things look different when you have
look different when you have a child Things look different when you have a child Things look different when you l
ave a child Things look different when you have a child Things look different when you have a ch
Things look di look different when you have a child Things look d
ifferent whe ifferent when you have a child Things look differen
when you h hen you have a a a child Things look different whe
ou have a you have a child Things look different when you have
Thrngs l ifferent when you have a child Things look differen
when yo nt when you have a chil Things look different when y
have a c erent when you have a c ld Things look different whe
you hav en you have a child Thi look d erent when you have
a child ve a child Things look fc ie have a child
Things ld Things look differe a child Things
look dif s look different whe Things look di
when you h t when you have a ch ifferent when yo
have a chi you have a child Thi hen you have a
child Things ve a child Things lo you have a hav
Things look d child Things look d you have a child Things
ook different nings look differ ave a child Things look dif
when you have fferent when you hings look different when yo
have a child en you have a ok different whehn you have a
Things look ild Thin c when you have a child Things
different have a child Things look diffeee
when you hild Things diffe-ent when you
have a ch ngs look different when you have a ch
d Things look di diffeeent when you have a child thing
s look sidde-ent whe erent when you have a child Things look
feerent when you have when you have a hav a child Things look di
ferent when you when Thing ou diffeee ou have a chil- things look different when you
ve a child things look diffe-ent hen you have a child Things look diffeent when you have a chi
ings look diffeent 2hwen you have a child Things look -ifferent when you have a child Things lo
diffe-ent when you have a child Things look -ifferent when you have a child Things look differn
you have a child Things look diffeent when you have a child Tvings look different when you have
hchild things lok different when you have a child THings look -iffe-ent when you-have a child
s look different when you have a child Things look different when you have a chil- THings look
iffe-ent when you have a child things lok different when you have a child things look different
you have a child TH'ngs look different when you have a child things look different when you have
chi-d things lok -ifferent when you have a child Things lokke ifferent when you have a child TH
look diffeeet when you have a child Toings look different when you have a child Things look di
erent when you have a child Things look -ifferent when you have a child things look different wh
you have a child Things look -ifferent w-en you have a child THings look iffe-ent when you have
Things look -iffe-ent when you have a chil- T ings look diffe-ent when you have a chil- THINGS l
diffe-ent when you have a child Things look diffe-ent when you have a chul- Tings look differen
when you have a child Things look diffe-ent when you have a child Things look diffe-ent when you
have a chil- T-ings look diffe-ent when you have a chil- things look diffe-ent when you have a
d things look diffe-ent when you have a child Things look diffe-ent when you have a chil- things
ook -iffe-ent when you have a child things look different when you have a chil- things
fferedt when you have a child Things look diffe-ent when you have a chil- Things look -iffe-ent
when you have a child things look different when you have a child Things look ifferent when yo

Pocket 1
Eleanor Eleanor (1979–)
Glass
2013

If I could learn to blow glass
into a very particular hollow shape
I would blow glass around an air pocket
the size and shape of a real baby,
as if the glass had surrounded
an invisible baby
up to the skin,
a baby made of my breath.

Glass doesn't blow that way
so I use a glass mould
made of two halves of metal,
fit the halves around a hot thick start
of molten glass and begin to blow slowly
the shell of glass
expanding and forming around
the absent baby
fitting inside the preheated metal mold,
a mold designed
with great realism and
in the manner of the fifty-cent plastic
Mold-a-rama figurine machines
of my childhood,
the kind one would find at
the Grand Canyon or

the koala tent of the zoo,
and one would put one's tiny hands
on the plastic bubble window and watch
as the two halves of the metal mould
were pressed together,
as brightly-colored liquid plastic
was injected into the mould
and machine-blown from within to cover
the mould's insides,
and the plastic dolphin or astronaut would take
shape, and then the two sides
of the mould would part dramatically
to reveal the figurine, which was then pushed
off its pedestal
by a metal arm
into a hollow space underneath,
where it could be retrieved,
smelling of hot plastic and
still warm after it had hardened
enough to hold.

I blow and blow the thick layer of glass
that expands to cover the invisible air baby
until its delicate hollow figure is perfectly formed,
and I remove the sides of the mould
and polish the glass around the baby that emerges,
and when the baby is perfectly, daintily life-like,
so full of detail it looks as though it might blink,
then I work huge layers of clear melted glass
around the glass around the air pocket of baby
until the perfectly clear outer glass encasement is the size of
a deep bathtub, heavy,
heavy and polished
with a slight blue-grey tinge the color of very cold deep water
so that it makes you feel claustrophobic for the baby
so that you want to dig out
an umbilical cord
so that you begin to breathe
shallowly so that you want, oh God,
to let in some air
to a baby made of it and tell me
what good would that do?

Copy

Copy 1: Cloud
Eleanor Eleanor (1979–)
Billboard, photographic copy, actual sky
2005

The sky is attached to the city
at its billboard.
I collect a picture of a cloud that is
right next to a billboard outside Detroit
an hour away from where I'm living
(the cloud grey and washed with the dirt of the air)
and make a grey copy
exactly the size and shape of the real cloud
and put it on the billboard.
This costs me $4,500 for three months.
The real clouds are free and endlessly
circulating. The city rolls through them
like a player piano, like endless
cashier tape. I see
exact copies of clouds I saw before
appear again in exactly the same place.
No cloud leaves a mark.

The city leaves a mark. Buildings
abstract the sky, blazon it
into its smaller parts. Buildings
advertise themselves on billboards placed
ahead of themselves,

outside of their space.
We see the billboard before we get the building
before we get the city.
The building is low, strip-malled or
the building is abandoned,
is in the process of getting ruined.
Abandoned advertisements are
both ordinary and retroactively portentous,
like looking at a picture of an already
dead man taken soon before his death,
or the already dead mother
of the already soon dead man.

Nobody new buys my billboard
when my three-months lease is up, so it stays.
Like real clouds, the clouds on my advertisement for clouds
start ruining, unraveling,
soon as I look away.

Copy 7: Needle
Eleanor Eleanor (1979–)
Steel
2009

Stabbed into the ground floor
of the grand lobby of the grand bank
on the street in the city
that houses all of the banks
and visible from the outside
through twelve stories
of window glass, this needle

is all grace and violence,
like the rocket connected to the earth
by a lift-off column of fire,
like the straightened neck of a long-necked bird
its head in the air to swallow
a still-writhing fish,

this needle makes you wonder
if the perfect curve one finds in nature
(think of the mathematics of shells)
resembles somehow the perfect curve
of perfectly manufactured steel
here. It does not.
This needle is
completely unnatural
every part of it
machine-made

and without seams and tall
so tall that you wonder how I even
got it in this building
(that is for me to know)

O common woman's-domestic-item
made masculine by scale,
tall, tall and hard-shelled, with the look
of something made to look exactly like
hundreds of thousands of other such things
manufactured by machines
that were themselves made by machines
so that this needle is so far removed from human hands
as to be an antithesis.
I know you want to touch its surface.

You cannot touch its surface.
There are guards, and videocameras,
this being a bank lobby,
and it is clear, completely clear,
that you would leave a print
like a baby touching a newly cleaned mirror,
that perfect fragility of sterile surfaces,
and yet the size and the expensiveness of the needle's diameter
makes you want to hold hands with other people, strangers,

and wrap around it with your bodies touching
only that might be too sensual
like riding spread-legged on the metal backside
of an atom bomb,

and the needle's vulnerable eye is suddenly something
you long to see the sun through
so much so that you wonder if I have configured it so
that the sun actually does peek through once a year
for thirty seconds on the shortest, coldest day
if you stand in the right spot
of the lobby of the bank

O needle, seamless and shined, near-mirror, up, up
and at the very tippy top
a real-life-sized camel-sized eye hole
for all the building's goddamned bankers
to pull themselves through.

Copy 2
Eleanor Eleanor (1979–)
Undisclosed materials and found materials
2006

I

In the glass display case
I have placed a leaf and
an exact copy of a leaf.
I have not indicated which
is the leaf.
The leaf is an ordinary autumn leaf,
a bit dry, green at its base,
its fingers brushed with yellow and red.
The copy of the leaf is green,
is brushed with yellow and red.
Each is smooth skinned with tiny veins
visible below the surface,
a hole wormed through
and browned on one edge,
with undersides dulled and greener.
I have made the copy of the leaf
out of materials entirely other
than the materials of the leaf and yet
you can't tell the difference.

II

In the second case, a whole bag of spilled leaves
and an exactly spilled copy of the bag, identical.
No trace of any glue.

III

In the window looking out of the gallery
are what appear to be two trees in the quad.
One of these trees is a tree,
one is a copy of a tree,
packed inside with a complicated system
of wires and painted metal clasps
so that the copied leaves release to the ground
at exactly the same rate
as leaves on the other tree.
And you stand at the window
staring pointedly at the trees
hoping to catch one in a gesture
too mechanical or too regular,
hoping one tree's leaves will fall
too quickly to the ground
due to some slight difference in weight,
some surface that catches the air differently,
due to the impossibility
of exact duplication,
but they don't. There is no difference.
As far as you can see.

Supplement 1
Eleanor Eleanor (1979–)
Cardstock and ink
2007–2011

Hanging note: Each printed phrase is to appear on its own placard. Each placard is to be hung directly under the regular placard of another person's art piece, free of charge, with or without the museum's permission.

This is a copy of another art piece.

—

This art piece stands in for the hole.

—

The artist worked on this piece for 10 years before declaring it permanently unfinished.

—

The artist looped the original film footage looped it and looped and looped individual parts of the original film footage until it was much longer and much more deeply boring until almost nothing of it was new.

—

Those wings are real.

—

Each one of those millions was made by somebody's actual hands.

—

People would steal the little pieces by walking over them in heavy shoes. The pieces would stick like bits of gravel to the soles.

—

That little bird in the corner represents God.

—

That little bird in the corner represents nothing it is an ordinary little bird.

—

Because guards never look at shoes.

—

Because museums want you to forget you have feet at all, or anything but eye.

—

The left wing is original but, if you look closely, the right wing is a copy of the left wing.

—

The artwork cracked all through on transit back from the museum, to the artist's delight. The cracks became part of the art.

—

The artist declared the art piece finally finished.

—

Later an impromptu screening would lead to an excess of boredom, which would lead to near-riots.

—

The artist's assistants made 290 others exactly like this one (which was made by the artist), each indiscernible.

—

The artist's assistant did all the painstaking coloring.

—

The artist employed 1,600 assistants for this art piece.

—

The artist made 24 more like this one but each on a different day or at a different time, tracking the light from one hour to the next.

—

The artist was so far removed from the work at this point, so given over to assistants, that his actual hands never actually touched the actual art at all.

—

The other 23 are scattered at museums and in personal collections across the world very few together anywhere.

—

The artist was a genius with faces but evidently struggled, if you look closely, with feet.

—

A smaller museum, many miles away, has an empty pedestal and placard waiting for the return of the stolen artwork near which you are currently standing in this far more famous museum.

—

Later, the artist would turn individual frames from the film into gigantic plexiglass sculptures.

—

Later, the gigantic plexiglass sculptures were somehow somewhere just altogether lost.

—

The crack starts small but opens wider, watch your step, opens until it covers the whole hall, floor turned chasm, until it's wide enough for the whole idea of the museum to fall in.

—

And so the art piece exists somewhere in between the museum here and the actual place in the landscape in the photograph there where this dirt and these rocks were dug up originally and where there's just a hole now.

Bird Bird Copy Bird
Eleanor Eleanor (1979–)
Magazine clippings, type
2008

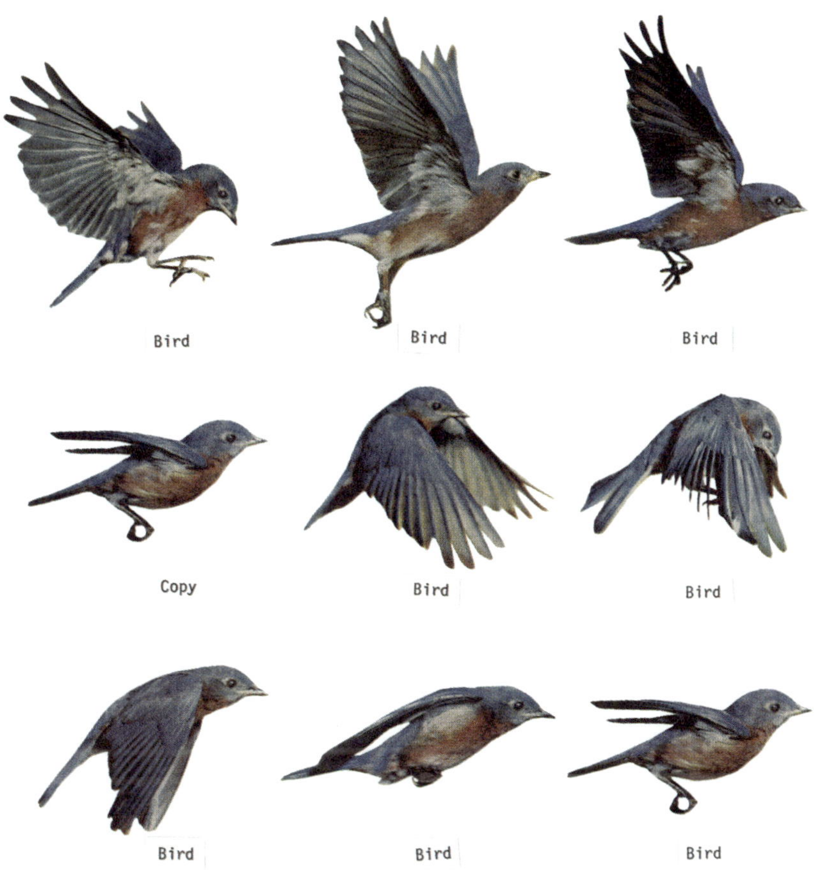

Copies 10–12
Eleanor Eleanor (1979–)
Various evidences
2016

> *after Janine Antoni,* Lather and Lick

I begin making sculptural copies of whole human bodies.
This has been done before—hyperrealistic naked people at a two times scale or
a guy asleep on a bench at an art museum who turns out to be made up,
or actual human bodies, dead and plasticized, insides made visible. But I
am less interested in trickery
than in materials and their relative durability.
I am myself a kind of material.
I am a material and my material
gets a little more ruined by every place I go.

> I make

a life-sized molded painted wax exact copy of me
and sit beside her in the Bonneville Salt Flats summer sun
in the exact spot and costume of my fashionable doomed wedding portraits
me and me in matching sundresses and folding chairs, the day hot for even hot
both copies melting
but melting differently. We sit
through the night and the next day sit
for 47 hours actually until I finally fall over smashing my cheek
into the half-inch of surface water on top of the salt.
The art is finished.

> Then I make

a sugar mold of me with colored-sugar-painted lacquer,

sit beside her
in the un-house-able back reaches of
the creeping swamps outside
my father's place in Florence, South Carolina. Soon
we are both covered in bugs
and practically kudzu. My bugs make my skin
swell and radiate out, red-puffed, fire-alarmed,
whereas the sugar me's bugs
make her melt and shrink in, her surfaces new-glazed
I take notes.

       I take
a copper cast perfect copy of me
and sit out from high to low to high tide
in the waves then pools then waves
on the Oregon rock coast near Cannon Beach
where I once burned a rut
(this was on my honeymoon)
in the palm of my hand with a kite string, where
I once sat with my father drinking honey-yellow wine, where
I once stood with my cousin an hour in the blank cold waves
so he wouldn't have to talk
to the people on the shore.
We sit, my copy and me,
saltwater crusting and eating out our open feet
and then the low-tide open air

rubbing a green-white glare
over both our salted faces, salted hair,
and then the water again when it comes back to get us.

All the copies are all ruined.
In the museum, what I show is the residue: wax melt, stained chairs,
hundreds of photographs, up-close sunburns, peeled skin, a salt-water sample,
its smell, a bug-pinned Styrofoam catalogue of common Southern biting insects,
two original itemized hospital bills, a pile of watered sugar and watercolor,
pressed greying vines, a tape recording of thick buzz and swat,
a diagram of the chemical alterations of salted metal over time, a distant sound
like inside the hole of a seashell, gigantic,
the paraphernalia of ruin, the fossil record, the evidence, everything
I can give you to show except
the actual there, except the me, except
the actual everything.

Copy 8
Eleanor Eleanor (1979–)
Metal, four motors, battery packs, robotic appendages, wires, latex, wax, paint, human hair
2010

After making various self-portraits and self-copies for various shows, I produce a version of my body I can really use. I can arrange her into a chair and sit on her back, and she's chair-like and strong, and she can hold me up. She corrects my posture. She rocks me to sleep. I can sleep standing up when I'm in her arms, as astronauts do in zero gravity, we take up less space this way (though we are double-sized), or I can sleep lying down on her, and as I move in my sleep, the version of my body can put her corresponding body part to mine to hold me up, surface of forearm to surface of forearm (her skin is mattress firm but with some give), ear to ear to cheek to cheek as I turn my head slightly in my sleep, and the effect is like what I imagine the effect of floating in air to be, like what I dream of when I dream I am floating in the air. Look I am holding myself up. Some kind of elaborate bootstrap. This version of myself is valuable, useful, would surely top the one million mark at auction if ever put to auction, which they say is a triumph for any woman, but I find I can't sell her the way I can't sell an ugly locket from my dead grandmother containing a lock of her hair from when it was still dark, from before I was ever born, from before my father was born, something I can hold to mark the hole, to mark the what's-missing-in-my-life.

So I produce another *Copy 8,* or rather, a *Copy 9,* a version of the version of my body I can really use, or rather, a version I can sell.

Self-Portrait as Empty Woman Shape
Eleanor Eleanor (1979–)
Magazine clippings, paint, poem
2016

wherefrom the shadows that are forms fall. // Wherefrom fall all architectures I am
—ROBERT DUNCAN, "Often I Am Permitted to Return to a Meadow"

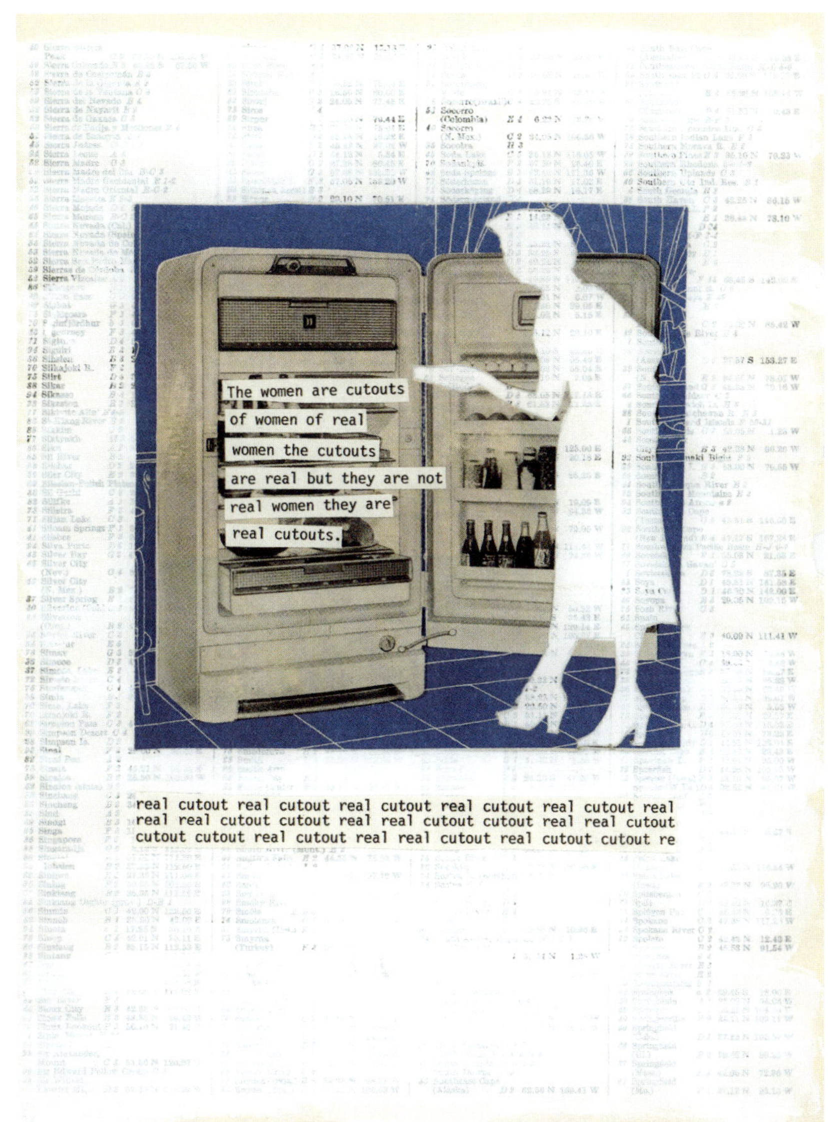

The women are cutouts
of women of real
women the cutouts
are real but they are not
real women they are
real cutouts.

real cutout real cutout real cutout real cutout real cutout real
real real cutout cutout real real cutout cutout real real cutout
cutout cutout real cutout real real cutout real cutout cutout re

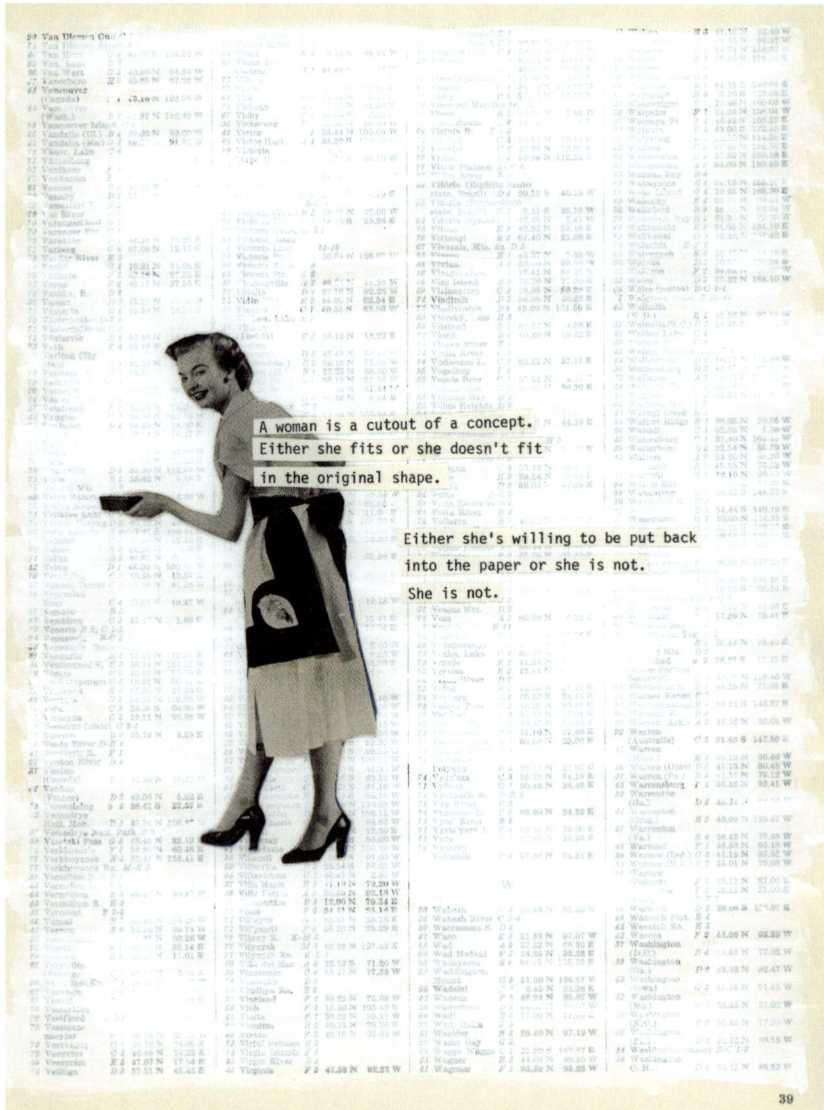

A woman is a cutout of a concept.
Either she fits or she doesn't fit
in the original shape.
Either she's willing to be put back
into the paper or she is not.
She is not.

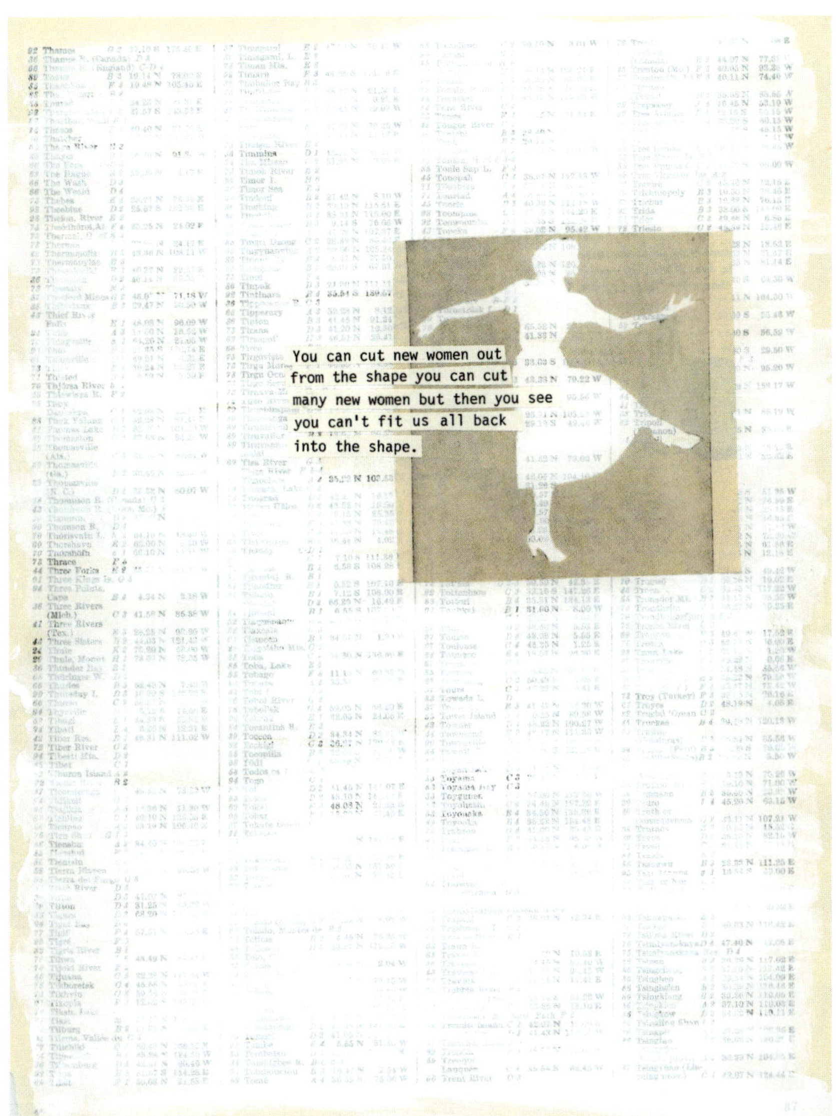
You can cut new women out
from the shape you can cut
many new women but then you see
you can't fit us all back
into the shape.

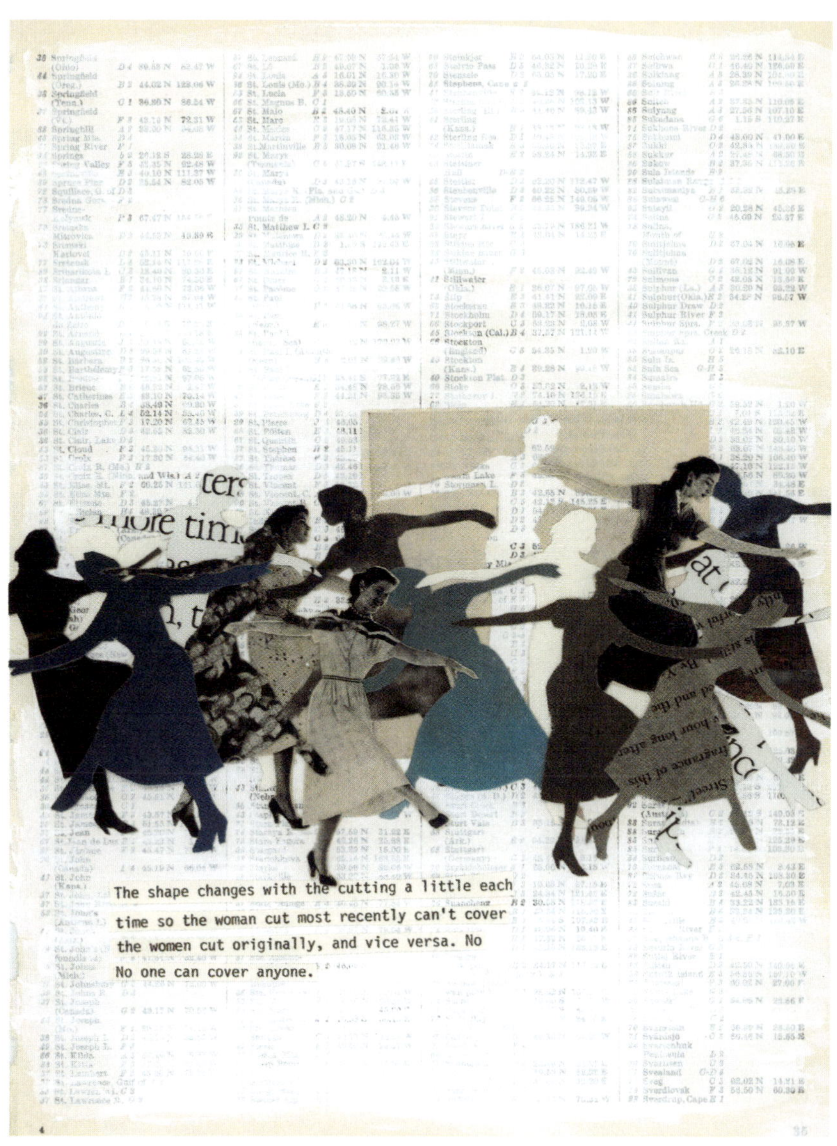
The shape changes with the cutting a little each
time so the woman cut most recently can't cover
the women cut originally, and vice versa. No
No one can cover anyone.

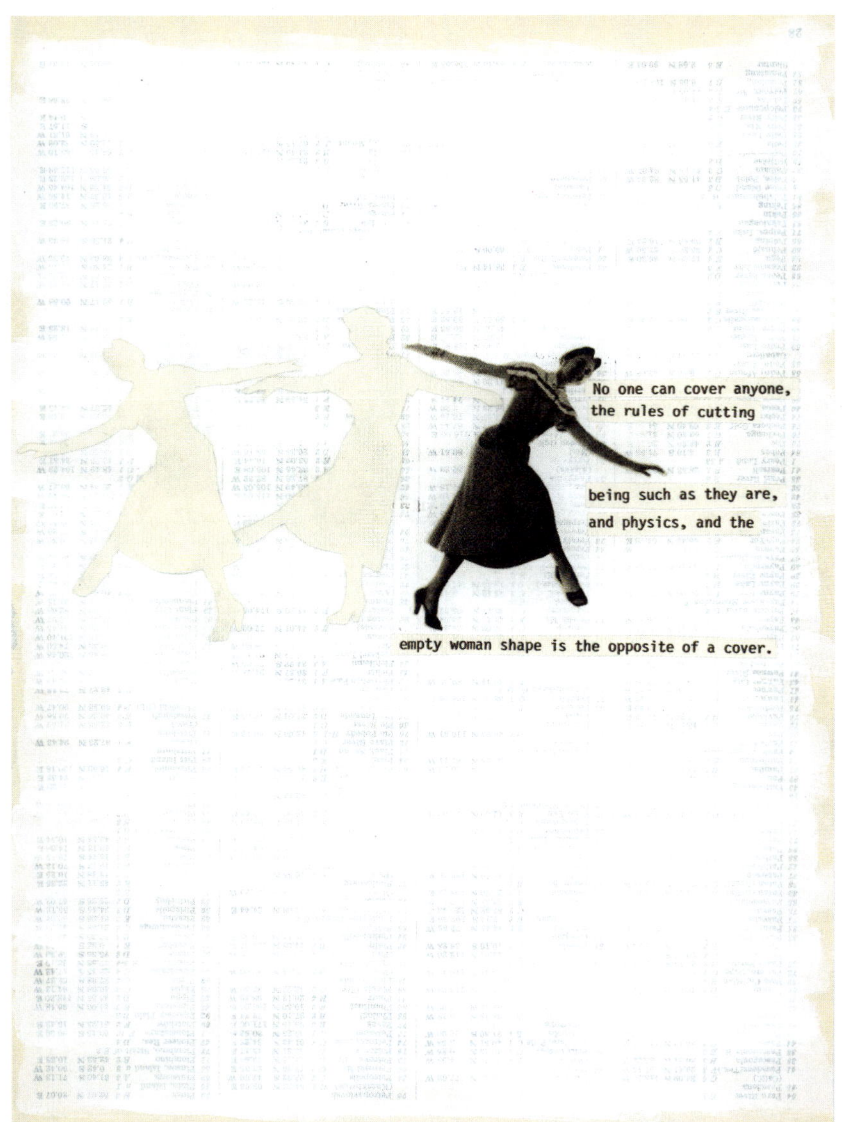

No one can cover anyone,
the rules of cutting

being such as they are,
and physics, and the

empty woman shape is the opposite of a cover.

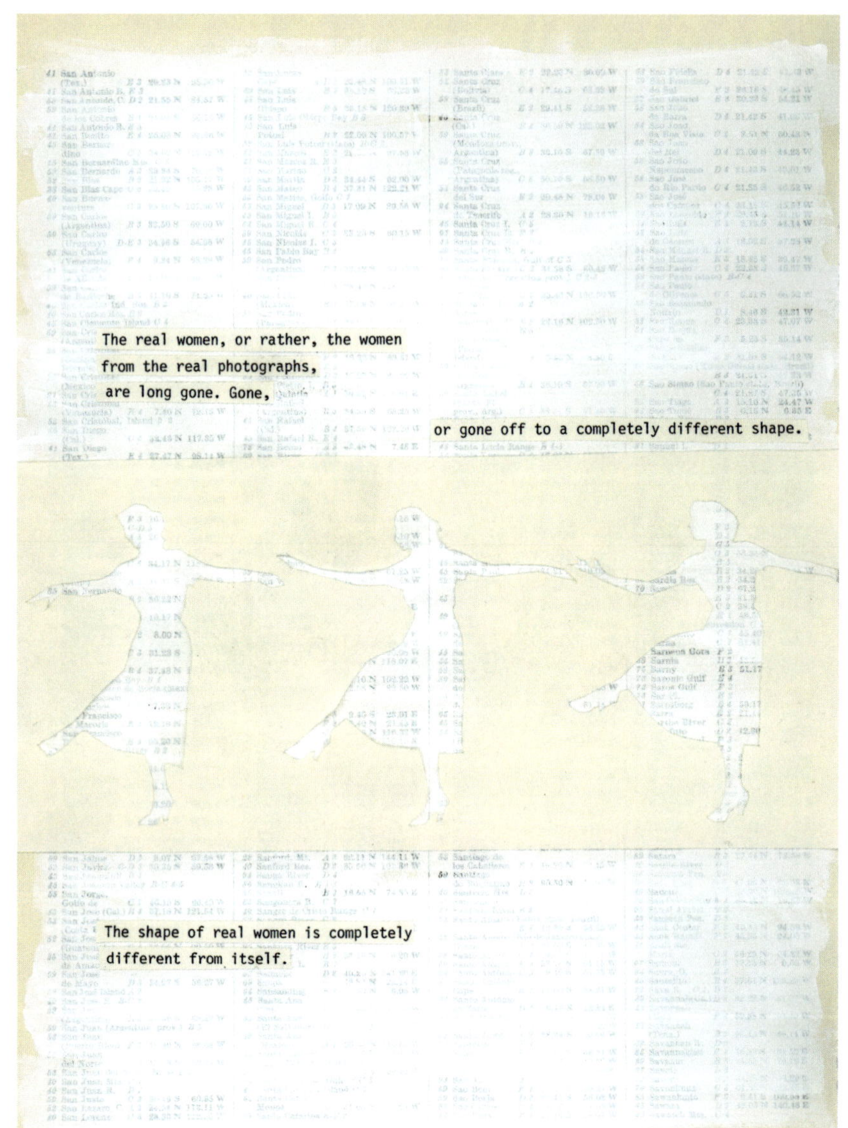

The real women, or rather, the women
from the real photographs,
are long gone. Gone,
or gone off to a completely different shape.

The shape of real women is completely
different from itself.

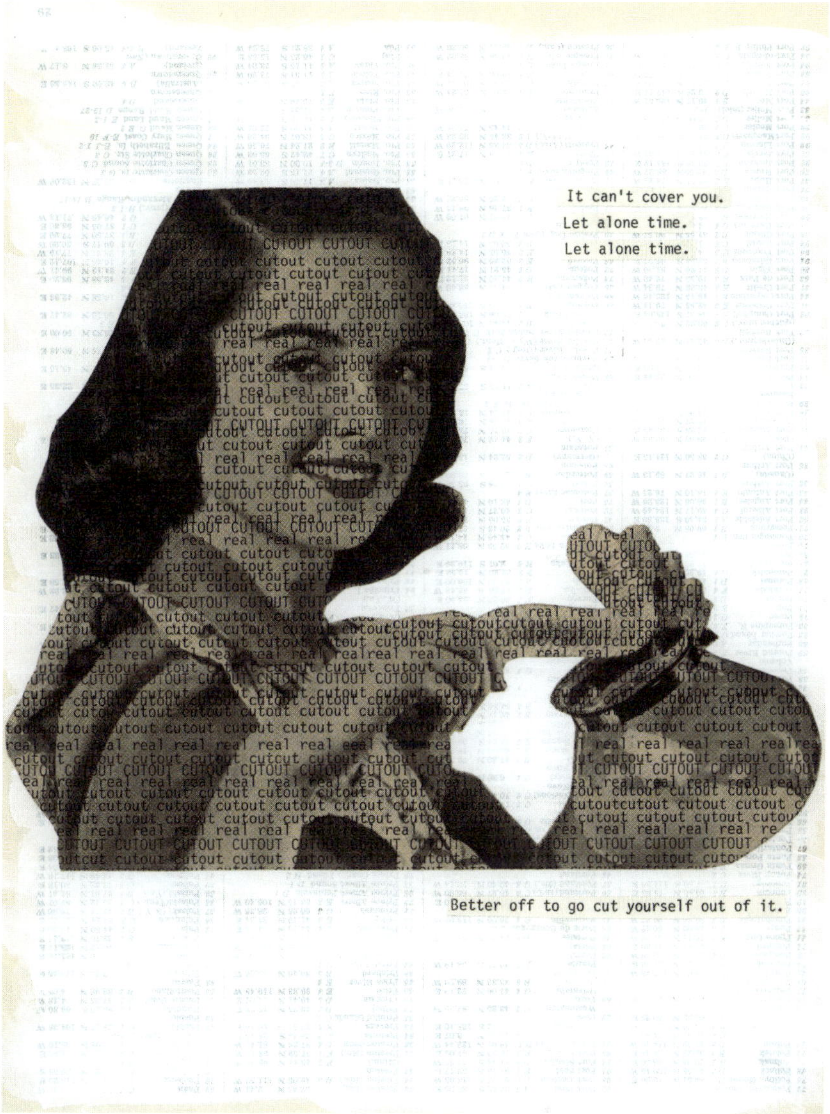
It can't cover you.
Let alone time.
Let alone time.
Better off to go cut yourself out of it.

PAGE LEFT INTENTIONALLY BLANK

Wife

Self-Portrait as Useful Domestic Item
Eleanor Eleanor (1979–)
Magazine clippings, poem
2014

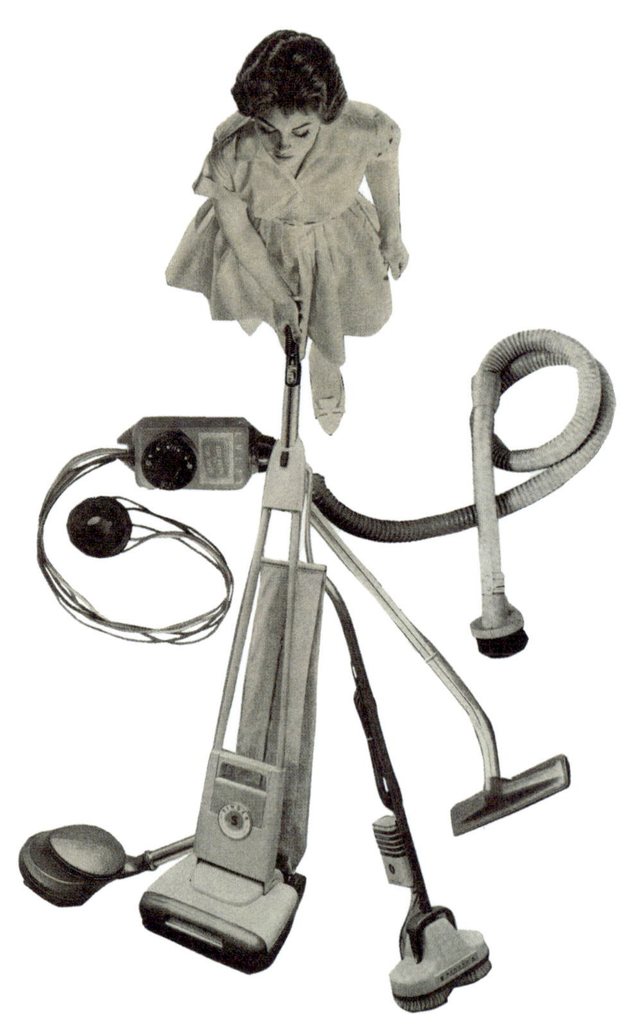

Use this nozzle for small messes, this tube for
larger, this buffer, this scrubber,
this shiner and gauge, this super deluxe
dusting brush telescoping wand retractable
power cord, yes, 50 percent
more suction complete with
separator tenderizer burner and cookie
press, egg beater and wringer washer and headlight,
did I mention it's self-propelled really
just another arm to have attached
to my own arm you see now how I am
the useful kind of multi-purpose tool.

Wife
Eleanor Eleanor (1979–)
Ceramic room, robotic arm, blowtorch, paper towels, hair
2015

I tie the word *wife*
on my jaw like a scarf
for my toothache.

Everything the wife has is blank—
walls, the bathtub, carpeting, couch, the kitchen—
especially the kitchen
with its white floor white
countertops white tile backsplash.

The white of a white kitchen can only be
theoretically clean.

In practice, there are specks.
In practice, fallen hairs, drifted dust.

Sometimes someone always spills the soup.
Sometimes someone always breaks the white plate,
or later steps deep onto a left sliver of soup bowl glass and thus
among other things
messes up the floor.

Even the light from
the cloudless sun is dirtied by old rain
left on the other side of the very window one looks through.

And anyway even if everything else was otherwise spotless still
my very eye would ruin it with looking
looking as I do out the eyehole of a
woman who is a wife who is a wife who
is a wife.

      I make
a pure white life-sized kitchen out
of a single vast surface of hard ceramic,
cooked in a larger-than-kitchen-sized brick oven,
a hard kitchen pulled from a mold,
a smooth fitted shell, the stove stuck
to the refrigerator to the wall all
hard white, inoperable, yes, but absolutely
clean.

I install a rigorous and complex
multi-surface-sensored video-monitored
alarm system such that
if a single hair, a single fleck
of a single hair, falls,
falls, then lands,

sudden red lights spin their terrible loudness like
storm sirens like

actual storms and
a mechanized whole blowtorch emerges robotic
on a metal arm from within the very wall and takes
aim and
incinerates the offending
whatever leaving
nothing not a scratch on
the heat-proof whatever
leaving no mark at all but slight
smoke residue that the arm
wipes clean
with a wet paper towel then wipes
the wet paper towel mark dry then
wipes it again.

The solid surface gleams
like a sudden tooth.

I am not in the scene.
There is nowhere here safe for a wife to stand.

Which is a metaphor for, which
is a metaphor, which
stands for something, you see, but
just what

I seem to have lost
to let slip
behind its stark,
its bone-like blank, its
equal sign, sharp.

Experiment
Eleanor Eleanor (1979–)
Metal, treadmill, buttons, psychiatrists, the artist
2009

Water is always available to me in a tube
extended from the ceiling.
I have bolted to the wall and floor behind me
long, thin iron spikes like the ones
in the dungeon of the castle in the film
with the handsome anthropologist
when the floor breaks away and he falls
and his length of rope, hastily tied
around his middle
is just shorter than
the distance to
the longest of the long spikes.
The psychiatrists in the corner
in the white coats and with their clipboards
are part of the art piece,
though they fancy themselves to be
conducting an experiment.

The children who visit the gallery
are often cruel, though in the way
a winter is cruel— without intention.
They have visited the natural history museum
where a button lights up a portion
of the exhibit on
quadrupeds of the Sierra.

They are merely experimenting with cause and effect.
So they push each button in turn
just to try them out
and I am glad when they leave.
Most people only push up to 3
and then laugh uncomfortably and push 1 again.
Some people never go past 1.

Then there are
the ones who enter the gallery
alone and wander around the periphery at first
as if with no purpose, never looking
my way until they stand
directly in front of me.
Then they look right into my eyes.
The guards are instructed
not to intervene.
The psychiatrists scribble furiously.
And then these visitors begin pushing buttons.
I know in a knot in my gut
they will push all the way to 5
slow, deliberate pushings across each button,
and then they will watch for less than a minute
with no change in expression.
Then they will turn and leave the room

casually, as if with no purpose
the sounds of my frantic movements
as if nonexistent, and they will walk
straight out of the art show
never once looking back over their shoulders
and they will go to meet their dates for dinner
or go home to their husbands and wives and children
or sit in front of the TV alone, faces blank,
microwave dinner grown cold.

Self-Portrait as If, Then
Eleanor Eleanor (1979–)
Magazine clippings, poem
2016

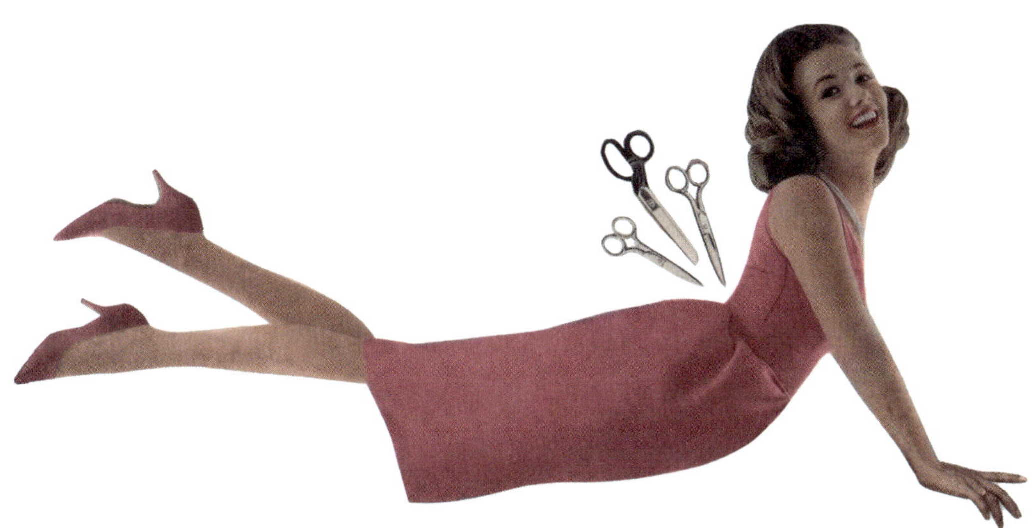

Yes, I am new sharpened
am on edge but
if I just
hold my arm right here
my legs just so, if I just
keep my face exactly, exactly
as it is —

There, you see, I'm
fine. I'm just, exactly, fine.

Happy Copy Happy
Eleanor Eleanor (1979–)
Magazine clippings, type
2016

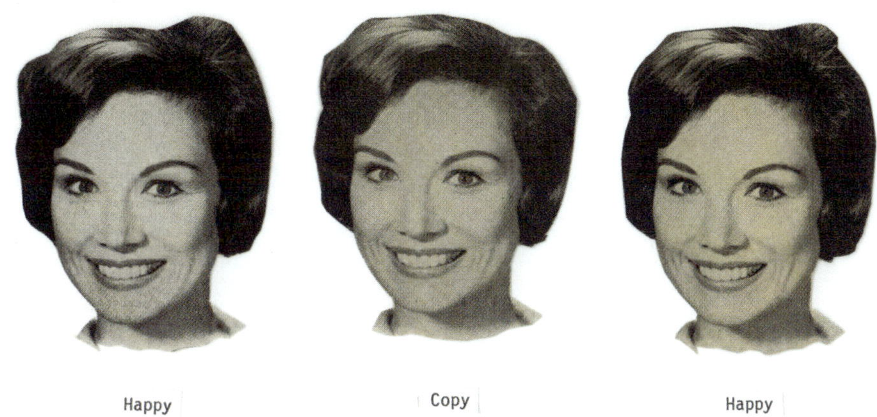

Disaster Thaumatropes
Eleanor Eleanor (1979–)
Paper and ink, silk sewing thread
2016

> THAUMATROPE: A scientific toy illustrating the persistence of visual impressions,
> consisting of a card or disk with two different figures drawn upon the two sides,
> which are apparently combined into one when the disk is rotated rapidly (*OED*)

On one side is the empty vase
on the other the pack of daisies, blank.
On one side is the robin redbreast
on the other the grey cage.
On one side the flank steak
on the other the lettuced serving plate,
or the tiger's open mouth and
the bent trainer's ever-reaching head.
You twist the thaumatrope string
two fingers on either end
and the centered paper circle turns and turns
till your eyes blink its two sides together,
a riddle, a blur,
a bit of wishful thinking, or looking,
a slipup, a q and a,
a catch, a metaphor turning,
tenor tricked into the actual car,
a substitution, a cancelling out,
a crossing of the bar,
on one side just half the letters
of *I love / you,* on the other side

every other missing piece
if you can just spin them together
fast enough by force,
a driving away of the nothing part
of the otherwise
perfect picture.
A collapse.
On one side a closet
on the other a housewife, crouched.
On one side a blank eye
on the other a darkening blink,
a run of black lash.
On one side my hand holds the blue bottle
on the other you snap it back up to my mouth.

I make a series of thaumatropes about disaster,
disaster and our little wide-eyed
house. On one side is the house
on the other a forked stick of lightening-strike.
On one side the house
on the other a wide sinkhole maws.
On one side the house
on the other a thick tornado path,
a sudden rip of grey.
Or this: Or even this:

On one side the house
on the other the tail end of a bomber plane,
early desert morning, a violent flash,
a sudden intake of air.
On one side the house
on the other a pillar, purple-orange,
a rocket launch without a rocket on top.
On one side the little bare house
on the other a nightmarish mushrooming,
a timelapse of impossible growth,
a nuclear treetrunk with great fiery
crown, spreading into unnatural green,
a brand new absolute sun, a razing
shockwall of bright hard air,
a fallout, a full
obliteration that covers
the whole thaumatrope side
and more, an utter rend
and flattening, and then a blinking
shut, finally, and forever, of the
blank house altogether.

Object/Subject 2: Looker
Eleanor Eleanor (1979–)
Digital movie camera, custom rig and stabilization, custom glasses.
2019

When I was a girl, movie score music
played in my head
as I walked down the street,
trailed by a camera lens,
also in my head—

the high-heeled exit shot, the pause
to look back, eyes flutteringly
soft, dark,
skirt breezed, leg flash,
cameras blurred and swooning.
Music swelled.
I pulled my head outside of my head
to watch. As a girl,
I used the windows of shops, the closed
doors of stopped buses, the sides of bus stops,
to see how I looked from outside.
I pulled the outside eye right into mine till
I could really picture me.

Girls watch people watch them and so
can picture themselves from away, two-placed.
This is a kind of art.

Whereas You are your own head, a site of looking-from,
making objects of everything you see,
girls are a reception center for looking,
pressed in on all sides.
How can I show this to you, you
who never thought of yourself
as to-be-looked-at.

                    I take
a hip-mount action-camera rig
and rig it to go behind a person, on wheels,
with the camera up slightly taller than you,
too close for comfort behind your head. Then I project
your own walking image, your behind, as it were,
onto the inside of your mirrored aviator shades in real time
so you walk down the street and see
not the street ahead, but yourself
walking down the street, two feet in front of you,
you're following too close behind you, see

that triangle of light
on your right shoulder, that taut,
the leaf blink of shadow on neck,
the shoulder breadth and back taper,
the inner leg flexion, the rub,

fingers brushing hair back, blink,
the softness of comb,
the hard-curled edge,
the music shifts, shifts
a sudden tall building throws
your whole back in shadow,
the startled hot light all swallowed, surface mouthed,
and then suddenly you walk back out again into sun,
all bright-edged, sun touching
every open piece of skin, look

what a piece of skin you are,
what a Piece, what a Looker.

You reach out, even,
to touch your
hair, to touch your own
not-really-there,
to feel if you are what you think you are, look,
what you see may be what you see, but,
like a girl, from another angle,
you are, you see,
another thing you can't have.

Self-Portrait as Device for Looking With 1
Eleanor Eleanor (1979–)
Magazine clippings
2014

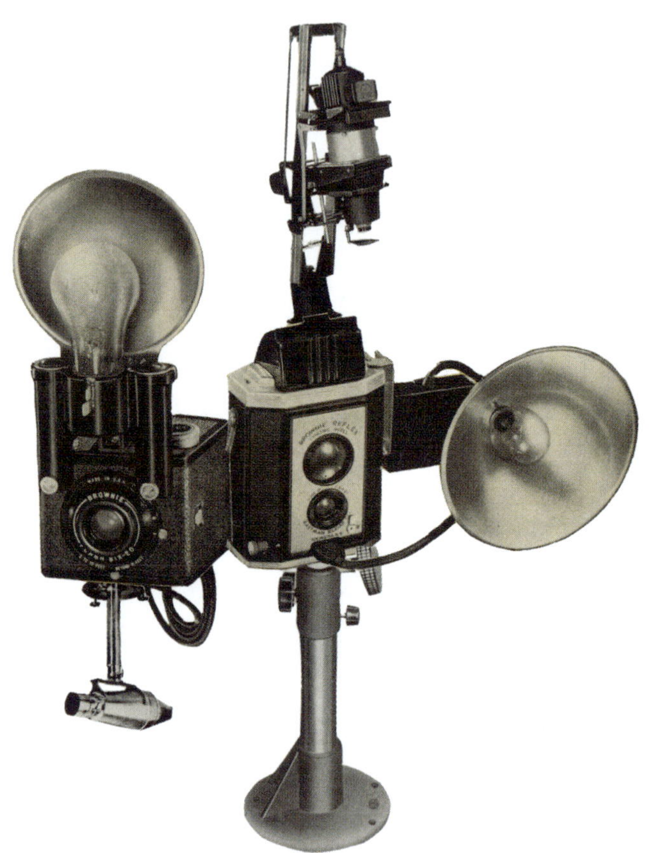

Self-Portrait as a Woman Washing her Face in an Advertisement for Faces
Eleanor Eleanor (1979–)
Magazine clippings
2013

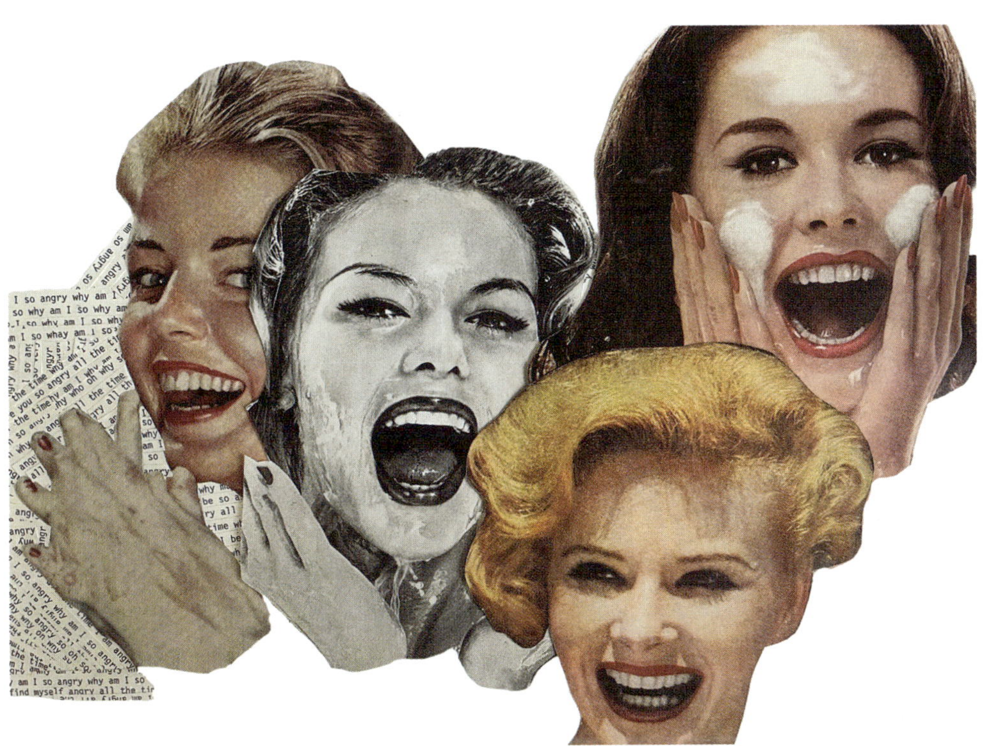

I so angry why am I
so why am I so why am
I so why am I so why
I so why am I so a
the you so angry am
the time why am all the ti
I so so angry all the tim
why who oh why
the time why who oh why s
I so
I so angry why
angry all
angry
angry all
time wh
be so
I be
angry why
the time
am I so angry why am I so
find myself angry all the ti

Musical Instrument Using Gravity 2
Eleanor Eleanor (1979–)
12 carnival-style High Strikers and mallet
2017

It takes great strength or great enthusiasm or great anger to hit an oversized hard-pine and red-rubber mallet at a red and white carnival-style High Striker Test-Your-Strength machine so that the metal puck slides up to strike the bell on top and causes the old-timey lightbulbs to sputter and spark. I have made a musical instrument out of twelve such High Strikers set up three to each side in a square to enable the fastest shifting from one note to the next. The lightbulbs run on electricity produced by the friction of the metal puck scraping up its metal track. Each bell is set to a different note in the scale.

I begin my training. I have neither great strength nor great enthusiasm, so I work on my anger every day. I think. I sit and think and think (nothing makes me angrier than that). Within one month, I am able to play five notes in a row of the little twelve-note song I can't get out of my head.

I get angrier. A month and a half passes and I have got to six notes on two separate occasions. The space in time between the hitting of the mallet and the hitting of the bell requires me to hold in my head two songs — the invisible song I play and the song I hear a half second later. I learn to keep two rhythms, like singing a round with myself. I get to seven notes.

I reconfigure the Strikers so their arrangement suits the song at hand rather than the general purpose of playing the instrument, my own highly specific typewriter QWERTY, my own spatial logic, an instrument made to hold one single song I did not write but that has by this point surely written itself into the very circuits of my brain. I perfect my aim, so the whole flat surface of the mallet hits the whole flat Striker pad as it lands. I use the momentum up off the pad of one Striker to raise the mallet up up the way a slipstreaming cyclist might, conserving energy, drafting on the bounce, and then the gravitational pull downward, intensified by the full downward force of my torso and biceps and back, flexed, as I slip my stronger hand down from halfway up the handle as it falls so that when the mallet hits (flat upon flat) both hands grasp its base for full violence, sending reverberations through the bones in my arms all up to my shoulders, sending the metal puck high.

I quickly jump to ten notes.

Every day I play the ten notes in a row of the little twelve-note song I can't get out of my head, once in the morning, once in the evening, every day I play. I can't get the eleventh bell to strike. I work on strength. I redouble my efforts at anger. I hire a masseuse for my perpetual back strain. I refill repositories of calcium shaken loose from my bones with a regimen of vitamin supplements. I do pull-ups. I do squats. And nothing.

Sometimes I can't even get to ten. Sometimes I can't even get to eight. When I'm very sick one day I can't even get to three, and it takes me all day to recover from the two I did get before trying again that evening, body racked. Every day I hit at the notes.

I hit at them I hit at them. Every day.

Painting with Holes
Eleanor Eleanor (1979–)
Canvas, oils
2018

This is a painting of a landscape
in the country
that is like the painting of the woman
where if you cover up
one side of her face
she looks angry and
if you cover up the other side
she looks tired.

The lake is calm or else
the lake is unfinished
is too much of one color of blue.
The sky is blushing or
the sky is opaque and watching a great fire.
The horse is panicked is
flying along and nearly
unseating his rider or
the horse and rider are
a statue of a horse and rider
in the town square.

The goats at the edge of the lake
are goats or are holes in the canvas
where the goats would have been
or where the goats chewed through.

The edge of the canvas
is a forest with a snake and
the snake is good like the word of God
or the snake is bad like the news
like eight children dead I just heard
or the snake never was a snake
but was a rope for climbing up,
a way out of the boxed corner
of the hurt painting, away.

Supplement 2
Eleanor Eleanor (1979–)
Cardstock and ink
2020–2024

HANGING NOTE: Each printed phrase is to appear on its own placard. Each placard is to be hung directly under the regular placard of another person's art piece, free of charge, with or without the museum's permission.

The art piece started out as a painting on canvas before it veered bodily, grew up and out. It weighed in the end more than a ton.

—

The collective weight of all these small bright-cellophane-wrapped candies is the same as the weight of the artist's lover just after he died.

—

To move the art piece from the apartment took complicated mathematics, six workers, and a forklift. Had to cut open the very wall.

—

This took the artist seven years.

—

This took ten.

—

Go ahead. Eat one.

—

Yes she said cut whatever you want to from my clothes. Just sat there.

—

The art is some combination of the sitting and the cutting.

—

The art piece is crashing imperceptibly into the wall with the help of its enormous mechanism. You can't see the crash moment by moment, but come back next month and its whole front will be smashed flat.

—

The sitting might seem passive, but after all, one difference between passive and active is sheer length of time.

—

The art piece started out as a column topped with the death mask of his child. Soon the artist covered over it with architectural features.

—

The mask was still there, of course, deep underneath.

—

In the end, it probably slowly killed her to make the art piece, full as the layered paint was of lead.

—

Tomorrow, the museum will add more candies to the stack.

—

Think of it as a corpse that's part flower bed.

—

The art piece started out in a single room but soon enough took over another then another then soon enough took over the whole floor of the apartment building.

—

She added and cut away, so that day by day it differed from itself, each new version a complete version, she said, but never quite what she meant to be the outermost layer of paint.

—

Think of it as jungle vegetation, ever covering and uncovering, soon as you turn your head.

—

The art had a life of its own.

—

The cutout figures collapse their layers into flat black silhouette, all surface. Because with silhouettes, you can't quite make out which part belongs to whom.

—

"What you see is what you see."

—

He found he needed still more space for the art piece. Cut a hole out up to the balcony.

—

"then what / is emptiness / for. To // fill, fill."

—

Each hidden layer a secret part of the surface of the work.

—

Yes in time the bombs destroyed the whole building.

—

Yes he burned every art piece he had made, baked the ash into cookies. Put an obit in the paper.

—

Yes he inventoried every single thing he owned, shredded it all up in a public display, then threw the garbage sacks unceremoniously out.

—

Didn't feel right to sell to some museum.

—

Think of the zero-sum as the art.

—

Because the actual art happened ten years back, twenty years back. Because what you see is merely the tail end of anything.

—

Although this machine looks like it's broken to pieces, it worked very well at its original purpose, which was to break itself to pieces.

—

All we have now is the photograph.

—

And he chainsawed through the whole house's shell, split it apart from itself, let the light come through.

—

She made a concrete cast of the Victorian house's insides before its great final tearing-down—an interior death mask, a turning inside out of its layers.

—

Because he never really stopped making the art piece, even after he fled. Carried the idea like a shell on his back.

—

The artist himself did not know what was inside the art piece. He had someone else put the thing in and solder it shut. All that's left now is the noise it makes when you shake it.

—

Think of the noise as the art.

—

And now he himself is dead.

—

In the end they rebuilt the shell of the art piece, the very outside layer, based on the photographs, but sans death mask, completely empty on the inside.

—

In the end they had to cut the original canvas loose, to excavate the interior of the art work in order to save the outermost layer of paint.

—

And it looked mostly the same.

—

And it was not the same.

—

The art piece is not the geometry textbook but the wind that
blows through it.

—

The art piece is not the glass but the light.

—

The art piece is not just the spiraled jetty but also the lake,
now creeping ever away.

—

And so the single art piece contains within it the entire life
and death cycle, right down to the worms.

—

"A fine wind is blowing the new direction of Time."

—

A famous artist's drawing used to be on the paper but it's
gone now, mostly, erased.

—

Think of the gone as the art.

Hall of Mirrors
Eleanor Eleanor (1979–)
Mirrors, glass, paint, video and projection equipment
2017

In one mirror you see a mirror. You see you. The first of many mirrors in the hall.

In one mirror a crack; in another a series of cracks.

In one mirror, where the eyes should be, a video of eyes.

In another mirror, a video of your own eyes, taken from just above the mirror, familiar and not, so your eyes look at your eyes askance, so that you cannot look yourself in the eyes without looking away.

In one mirror, no eyes—just a strip of mirror pointed elsewhere where the eyes should be.

In one mirror you see the mirror on the wall directly opposite, through which you see you and your mirror, through which you see the mirror on the wall opposite, through which you see a forever of mirrors.

In one mirror, your actual face, not the mirror image of your face you're used to, which feels like hearing your own recorded voice.

One mirror is frozen in place, as if glitched.

One mirror a half second late.

In one mirror, our joint moving video faces, yours and mine, in composite love child.

In a side room, a room of mirrors at triangular funhouse angles, all reflecting you except the one containing a video image of me and not you, which is to say containing a startle.

In one mirror, a little circular mirror in the wall behind you reflects, if you look very closely, the artist who is painting the scene.

One mirror is handheld and heavy as a weight.

One mirror is entirely blank. (Through the use of smoke andetc.)

In one mirror, placed insignificantly three from the end, behind a two-way mirror, I sit, there in person, half-visible in a half-lit room, waiting as people visit my art piece, waiting for You. When you look you see you, you see me, both by half.

That's when I get up and go.

I walk out of the door of the little room and out of the hall. I walk out of the Staff Only corridor and out into the grand museum lobby. I walk out of the rotating glass door and out of the grounds and out through the ceremonial cast-iron gate and out onto the street. I walk out and further out till I walk to the edge of the city. I walk out of the city out of the state. I keep walking. Always I walk out. I'm walking away from you always.

Self-Portrait as Empty Spot

Portrait Piece
Eleanor Eleanor (1979–)
Oil on canvas, half skeleton, papier-mâché, cloth strips (various)
2019

I painted a portrait of You
in secret three years ago, I who
never paint anyone I know. In it
you are handsome, as you are,
and also absolutely paper blank,
also as you are. I made it painstakingly
bland, I made it lovingly, obviously
I cannot let it stay or stand I must
do something. The question is
the what, the way out.

              When accused witches
"stood mute" and would not face
the blaring court and would not plead,
then heavier and heavier
and heavier stones were pressed
on their fragile human
chests—"as much as [they could] bear, and more" per
one account—to compel them.
And if they still would not then plead
it took hours or even days till
the great bone collapse of
snapped-ribbed end or else
till there was no more room for even one
single slight breath.

I make a paste 1/3
heavy glue 2/3 drywall joint compound
and mâché my portrait
of you onto an antique physiology classroom skeleton
damaged but made of actual human bones
I had been saving for something special
part Fayum portrait part pippy doll
ugly all on a wooden base.
I begin to tear cloth strips. I have a lot
of our old sheets monogrammed and towel sets
throw blankets soft pillows and
clothes, I have clothes
loads of shirtsleeves and trousers sweaters
long skirts short skirts old gowns and tights
men's striped socks coats camisoles piles of underclothes
and some gigantic scarves and shawls and
I am headed in the direction of summer, no
need to stay warm, I have
time. I tear the canvas tent and sleeping gear,
backpacking pack cut up and grocery sacks and the covers
of every cloth covered book, even the ones
I want to keep, the dear, and wash rags and leather
work gloves, boot trim and my long-clutched
childhood stuffed turtle, I tear
every last stitch of loose cloth I have left,

every thread your least breath may have touched,
and mâché it airless on top
of the rest, a leaning tower, a great smoke
stack, and then,
because enough is not enough,
I start on other kinds of cloth — the custom
curtains tablespreads rugs slipcovers
ripped right off, I begin
to tear out the carpets from the floors,
their filthy pads glued alongside,
some green cloth wallpaper, the skins
of the armchairs and sofas and ottomans all
smashed together with mâché paste.
I move the whole thing to the barn,
then use a ladder, teetering and taller,
then just stand on the second-floor loft.
I scaffold my stack with spare barn wood,
rigged to the sidewall,
get it heavier and heavier
and heavier till one day I hear, finally,
the strong ribs give way
and crack shut, the clean snap
of a spatchcocked turkey, palm
to sternum, pressed impossibly down,
my skeleton flattened like the bones

of archeological digs
crushed nearly two-dimensional
by the weight of whole
epochs underground,
by the weight of time.

                    In the gallery,
I lay the portrait
3 rooms long,
straight through
the doors, on its side,
with gigantic metal grape press screws
on tip and tail, holding its layers together, and still,
by the end of the run,
I find there is more
I have to add—
and still, by the end, I find
I am not sure if it is a portrait
of you or of me.

Heart 2
Eleanor Eleanor (1979–)
Mixed media (tuning forks, megaphones, windmill, catapult, volcano, bathtub, confettied heart, tissue-paper flowers, flamethrowers, pianos, etc.)
2019
     after The Way Things Go, *by Peter Fischli and David Weiss*

I give the boot on a stick a push.

     The boot circles round and kicks the light switch on, which, as the open bulb grows hot, melts the balloon full of red red paint, which drips down to fill up the glass precariously balanced until it tips over and breaks, tripping a wire on its way down,

     and the wire sends a spoon attached to a little weighted car down a ramp, and the spoon hits against strategically placed tuning forks in different notes as it travels down, and the tuning forks are each pointed toward a red and white megaphone set at full volume, and the megaphones serve to amplify the little 12-note tune that I can't get out of my head,

     and when the spoon car gets to the bottom of the ramp, it smacks into a striped target, which knocks a red bowling ball onto an oversized inflated black plastic bag, which releases its air into a long silver tube in a burst, causing the white canvas windmill at the other end of the tube to turn,

     which tips the wooden see-saw structure so that it releases its 1,000 one-inch rubber balls in various shades of red and pink and grey down a 25-foot wooden plank, and then into a metal chute, where they line up and twist and turn their way, roller-coaster-like, to the bottom of the track, picking up speed all the while,

     and at the bottom, they split into two tracks and collect in two separate tubs attached to two separate strings that will only pull once enough balls have accumulated in the tubs, given enough weight, one string attached to a trip wire attached to an oversized match, which quickly strikes against its measure of sandpaper and lights on fire, and the other string attached to the safety catch of a tightened, loaded bow above it,

and the string slowly, slowly, as the waiting match burns down, as the tub fills with one-inch balls, pulls slowly at the safety catch until it, quite suddenly,

releases, letting loose the paraffin-soaked arrow, which passes through the flame of the oversized match and lights up as it shoots just feet above the heads of the seated spectators in the outdoor garden of the art museum, over, across the open space, grazing on the other side of the crowd a wick attached to the paraffin-soaked cardboard mannequin,

which bursts into a flame that lights all the attached oversized sparklers from their shortened bases, and they burn in reverse, outward, and the mannequin sags, and the mannequin gets infinitesimally lighter, as the sparklers drop their ash to the ground and as the chemicals react and burn away, so that the enormous and sensitive scale holding the sparklered mannequin on one side becomes outweighed by the enormous pile of inflated red beach balls on the platform on the other side of the scale and slowly lifts into the air,

and a metal ball rolls in a track along the edge of the platform and catches in a pocket on one end of a wooden plank,

causing the giant catapult full of red-dyed baking soda on the other end of the wooden plank to fling its contents in the air and, upon hitting the vat of red-dyed vinegar in the center of the giant papier-mâché model of a volcano, to bubble up over the edge and through a rugged papier-mâché channel painted to look like rock on the side of the volcano,

and the fake lava flows into a water wheel, which turns and turns, and its turning untwists a 50-foot length of rope from around a pole high above the crowd, out on the end of a crane,

       and the pole is attached to the side of a bathtub full of confetti made from
hole-punching-to-pieces every letter or postcard You ever sent me every photograph
I have of You every scrap of film every original thing every only-copy-that-exists and that
might hurt to lose,

       and the bathtub turns,

          and turns on its pole,

              and upends its contents onto the crowd
as 12 pianos each tuned to a single note drop in succession,

              a literal kind of surround sound,

                  playing
the little tune I can't get out of my head,

          as confetti cannons shoot red tissue-paper flowers
into the air,

   as the tissue-paper flowers pass through the blaze of the flamethrowers,

                  four of them,
strategically placed,

       as they light one after the other and burn completely to ash before
landing gently and harmlessly alongside the confetti on the heads and shoulders of the
crowd in the museum garden 50 feet below.

One-off 1−7
Eleanor Eleanor (1979–)
Paper, string, metal
2024

> "It'll have to be something that I'll miss"
> —WILLEM DE KOONING to Robert Rauschenberg re: "Erased de Kooning"

You press your forehead as instructed
into the paper forehead pad above the eyeholes
of the paper art machine
mounted inside the wall so
its eyeholes are flush.

As you press, a wire trips. The tiny paper curtain lifts.

Behind it, a pop-up book on a spring
tunnels back into the wall,
all hidden strings and action origami,
simple machines, a shift and flutter,
tiny bits of folded paper on moving tracks,
a clicking sound, a miniature mechanized sculpture
arranging its wings.

Inside, a tiny pop-up copy of an art piece I once made
and loved, one cut right from my heart, but that was
only so-so in terms of objective quality, so that I
had to cut it out from the oeuvre, remove it from the Catalog,
discarded, abandoned, kicked shut.
Each art machine in the series is unique.

Perhaps, when you look in, you see a paper circus tent
that folds out to reveal a packed paper crowd,
and high above, a woman from a dream I had,
her identical twin daughters balanced on a bar
across her sequined shoulders as
she rides a glittered paper bicycle on
a paper tightrope wire, rides Forward Forward. Pause.
Backward. Pause.

Or perhaps in the paper eyeholes of this particular pop-up machine
you see a Virgin Mary
with a gatefolded paper door on her growing belly
that opens like a myth into vineage,
paper grapes overripening before your eyes, tendrils
wrapping the now-visible unborn baby round,
a sudden blood gush of paper wine.

Or maybe a motorbike sputtering up flecks of paper gravel behind it,
Your motorbike, yes maybe yours, the very one from way back when,
only papered entirely over.

Or maybe a mechanical hand, writing you a real last letter,
just-readable upside-down,
then creased clean with a tiny bone folder,
then tucked in a neat, tiny envelope. Yes,

it's all yours, this whole tiny stage,
carefully made of moving paper parts.
I made it just for you, not You, but you whomever,
you the viewer.
Everything you see here. Pause.

Then you hear the paper sliding again, above, below, surfaces slipping
behind other surfaces, a planned rearrangement along a fixed track,
a foregone conclusion.
And suddenly
a flash of fishnet legs, loose spangles
and bicycle spokes, a torn hinge,
paper gears outbiting their teeth,
a grape squeezed right from its skin,
the motorbike driving ever away, small and smaller,
volvelles spinning, the letter ever dropping through a slot,
a visible whoosh, a breeze on your actual eyeball.

You pull your eye away from the paper forehead pad from
the paper eye holes instinctively,
pull your head away and,
in pulling, trip another wire, thus
loosing, behind the wall,
two heavy, hard, gigantic blocks of solid steel,
which snap shut and flatten

out, irrevocably,
the tiny fragile perfect paper single-use art machine, now
destroyed right in front of its only witness,
its only ever set of eyes,
now all used up, smashed, now existing, just think of it,
the entire art piece
existing now only in your
shut-tight own head.

Chronological Still Life
Eleanor Eleanor (1979–)
Birds, beasts, flowers, wire, acrylic paint on canvas
2021

The packed petals, thin-velveted and loosed
on the table, pink-streaked, irregularly ridged,
the fish scales half stripped,
the abandoned orange, its split pith,
its visible squeeze and gloss,
the bread knife's slit, the chipped crust pressed
with mince, the untidy feathers
and pomegranate seeds, the three cheese slabs,
stacked, one colored like a hard salmon side,
one sculpted and lard-like with a soot-cream rind,
one most resembling plain white soap, only soft
with dark green patches like pond bilge,
the greying-already oysters,
the slick-surfaced wine glass angling light, look

I want to eat it too,
fast, before it goes, but more than that
I want to paint it—
not the idea of it, hardened into
a version of itself that sits still,
not a stand-in for abundance, or for impending death,
not a rich man's rich reflected back,
not a play on surfaces, or a trick
to make your eyes make your mouth water, no
I want to paint with

the actual fruit, here on the table,
not a copy but the thing itself—
per Jack Spicer, *to make my poems
out of real objects. The lemon to be a lemon the reader
could cut or squeeze or taste.*

                                    I cut
a cross section of the lemon,
edge it with some yellow paint
and sew it on the canvas.
Onto the seedhole of the cantaloupe slice I wire
seed after seed from behind, surface-slopped,
but fairly sturdy, so the pulp stays put
in the ragged green-grey of the patterned rind.
The peony I pound flat like a chicken breast and glue
part to part from behind, petal to sapel to filament,
and the grape bunch, likewise, I burst, like a pregnant
smashed spider, its tendriled leaves curling.
And the purpled onion flower,
and the whole lobster tail.
My still life is pressed and firmly attached to its canvas
by an architectural underbelly so it's
not two-dimensional exactly, but still
not three, partial, a foot
in each of two rooms. Pause. Then

the fruit flies find it, even in the clean
of the gallery. Then the melted fruit overflows its edge
and the canvas takes on water. Oh,
the cow tongue smells really bad.
Maggots emerge from the goose wing joint,
and spread, breed, and eventually fly off.
The lemon wrinkles and eventually
kinks its neck. Petals go brown and fall,
flaking like pale pink paint.
Various molds mold over time,
various curdlings organize themselves
into soft color groups. Thus

the painting happens
in live chronological order
for a few weeks and months until it
stills, finally. Starts to take on dust.
The smells calm. The bugs lose interest.
And the hardening that happens
happens because of time, not because of me. Still,

long after the wine dries into a red film
of itself, I know I could taste it
if I tried. And after all this time, I find
my tongue still perks at what my eyes see,

my art still feels like food, after all this time, I find
I want to try it.

Covers 2
Eleanor Eleanor (1979 –)
Yarn, yarn-covered things
2022

I learn to knit so I can knit covers for things, easy things at first covers for my hands covers for
my feet for my head and neck soon I am making covers for friends as well I am adept at
covering I cover handles on doors I cover the tops of pots, themselves covers, covered with knit
yarn, I cover things for my daughter, small things, I make a cover for her eye and a cover for
the eye of her doll I make a cover for her doll covering the whole thing except for the eye, for
which I have already made a cover, I cover her dollhouse in great patches I connect the patches
I am on a roll, I learn to knit in my sleep with the aid of a sleep knitting machine I cover my
bed over and over again at night I become more and more adept until I can knit covers for
myself as I walk, slow business to be sure but faster and faster for I find I need always to be
under cover everywhere I go so I knit the cover and trail it behind me to cover where I've been.

Self-Portrait as Mythological Figure
Eleanor Eleanor (1979–)
Magazine clippings, poem
2023

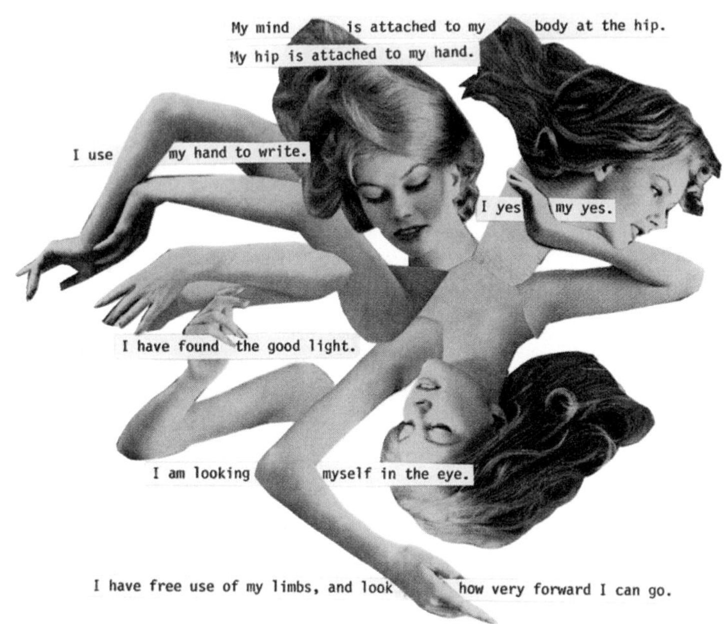

Painting of an Empty Spot
Eleanor Eleanor (1979–)
Oil on canvas
2024

The women are wax-legged and slight-smiled.
They are waterlogged in a too-small boat. They are looking
over their shoulders from under parasols, from under
thin coronets set over loose hair,
a dark flip of lash.
They are holding their babies or bellies, their breasts
or silver-carved hairbrushes, their John the Baptist
serving platters or
apple and snake combos they
are catching the spear-spurt blood of Jesus, look
that woman is being bitten in the back
of the neck by a lion the lion
is trim and remarkably well-manicured but
that makes little difference to her.
The women are sick of the lion,
of the messenger angel, are sick
of the dumb bird, of the nipple-dragging baby
or the fast-advancing army, are sick
to death of slipping into the armhole
of someone else's story, sick of rending
their own faces with their nails,
of dying right in front of you, getting kicked
out of paradise, or washing again the baby
or someone's feet with their hair, the women
don't like the washing,

don't want to stand in the damn sea-
shell, want the angel to quit with its happy stab,
want out of this yank of wind, the women,
freezing off their fleshy thighs and angled toes,
their dimpled bums and identical parted
mouths, freezing naked yet holding inexplicably
multiple yards of loose heavy fabric, the women
are so goddamn sick of throwing their arms
in the air like empty shirtsleeves
as some thick man drags them off again,
or their sister, or their twin, sick
of the endless looking-in-the-mirror,
of sitting quietly on a great velvet
whatever furniture item under the staggering weight
of their looped and plaited
and tucked and curled and caught tight
own hair, of the neck cuff the size
of a dog recovery collar, pearl inlay
with peacock embellishment, the guild
and encrust, the filament and bead,
the corset and cleave, the complex floral
arrangement, the entwine,
the flowers growing up leg and
spine, the angels throwing petals at their hair,
the air, the slick-tipped

fur wrap and black choker, the heavy
gold brooch and chain, always the chain,
their own candle-rich red-couch-draped
dresslessness, the naked leg sprawl, the open
skin, the tutu, the pedestal, the cooking pot, the child's cry
just out of earshot, the sun umbrella,
the sun itself, O, goddamn
sick of the head-hammering halo
and the accompanying wings,
how they drag
every moment they aren't flying, which is to say
every moment.
The women are sick to death of it all and so
I have painted instead of the women just
the piles of stuff, torpid, unpeopled,
the piles and the empty space,
which has just now been vacated by
the women, yes, you just
missed them, the women
have just left, have sprung, decamped,
got the hell out of Dodge, have turned
their backs, you know, on you, which is to say
the frame altogether, yes,
the women finally have finally
stepped goddamn out.

Clouds
Eleanor Eleanor
Acrylic on canvas
2005

This is a painting of a woman.
She is naked in her kitchen.
I paint her some clothes, a dress
and a long sweater with a belt,
some high-heeled boots.
She is still cold.
I paint her a winter coat with a woolen collar
and expensive gloves. The gloves
are red cashmere on the inside
and soft black leather on the outside.
I paint her hands into the hearts of the gloves.
I paint the new red rug leading out
of the kitchen, I paint the whole apartment,
I paint the door.
I paint its thick locks, its gold chains,
I paint its layers of paint. I paint
the outside of the door, the peephole,
the hallway with its hotel carpeting, I paint
the wooden stairs and the mailboxes.
I paint the stoop.
I paint the bicycle tied to the gate.
I paint the length of the street, and I
paint in trees. I paint a leashed bulldog walking
the length of the street.

The bulldog turns a corner.
I paint the corner, the whole city block,
and the next block, and the next, I paint
the thoroughfare out to the sea.
I paint the whole downtown. I paint
the cityscape as seen
from a fishing boat 3 miles out.
Airplanes circle through clouds
in the sky waiting to land.
People sit in tightly gridded
configurations in the airplanes, reading
and hurtling through space at unthinkable speeds.
This is a painting of the people in the airplanes.
This is a painting of clouds.

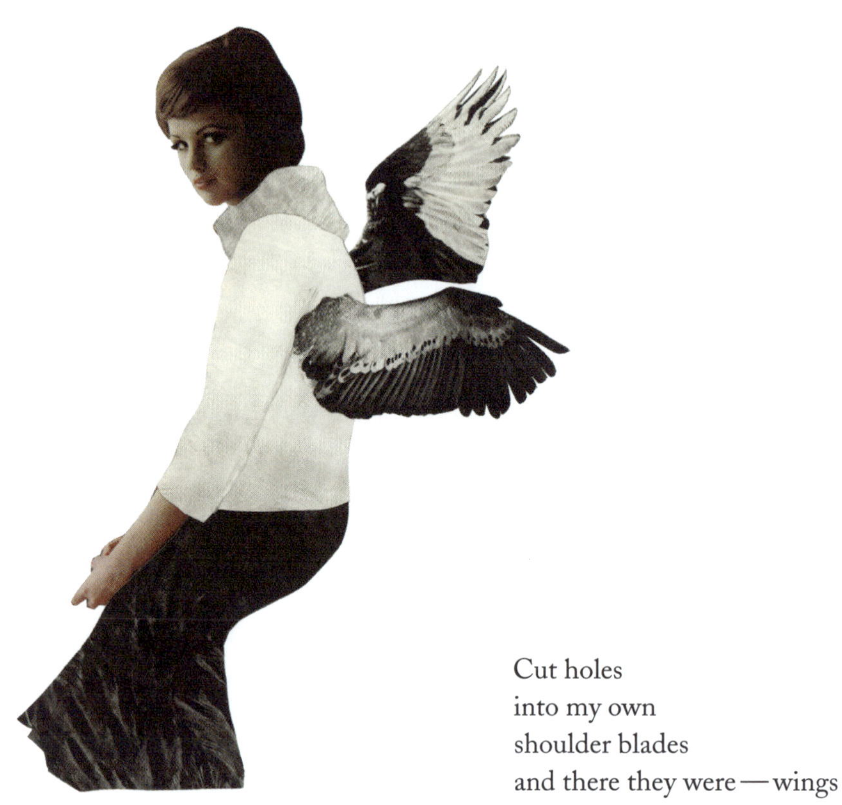

Cut holes
into my own
shoulder blades
and there they were — wings

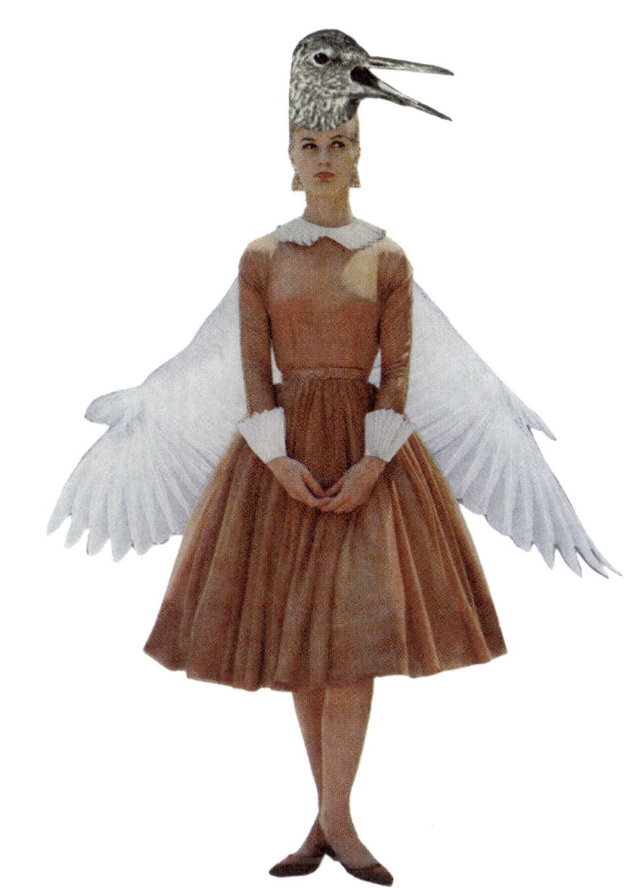

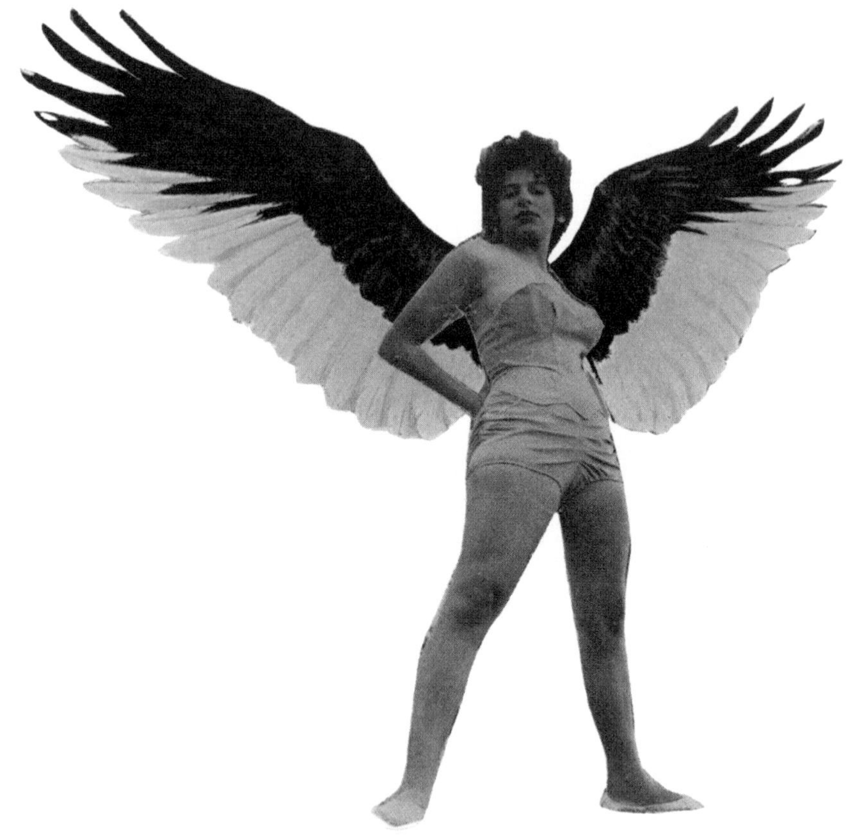

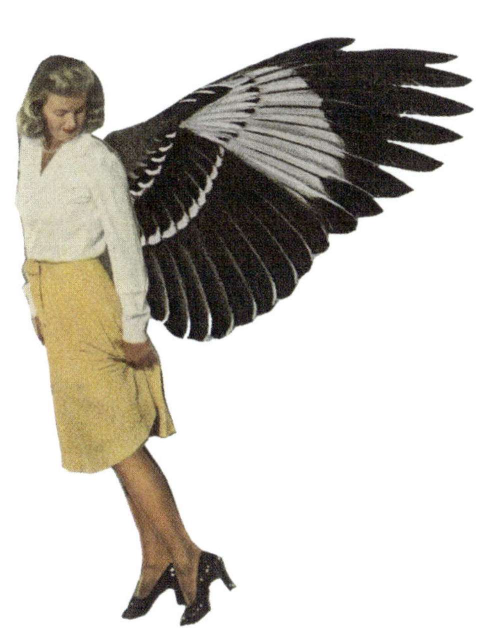 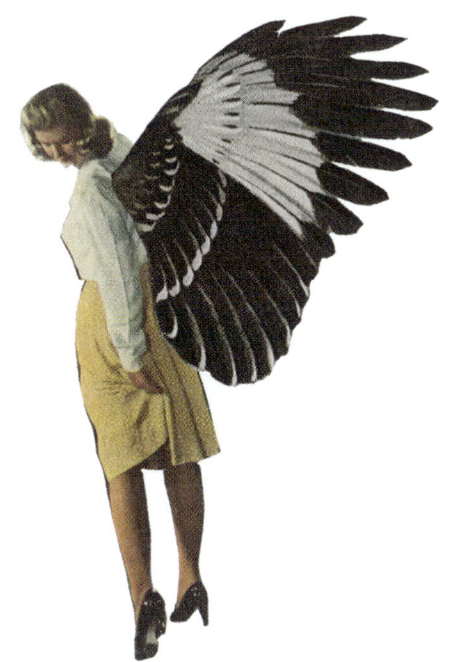

stood to the side
of myself and pulled, and pulled,
a split cell

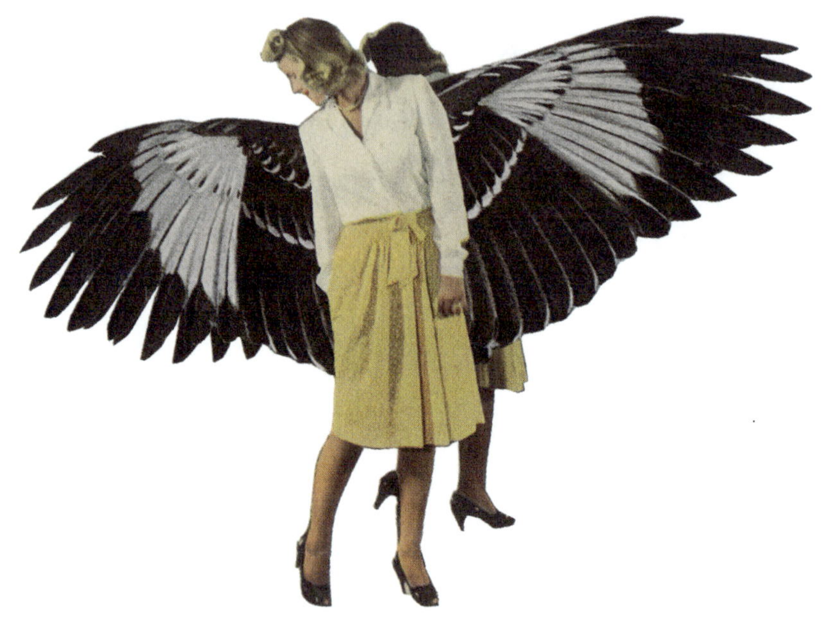

left behind a copy, husk

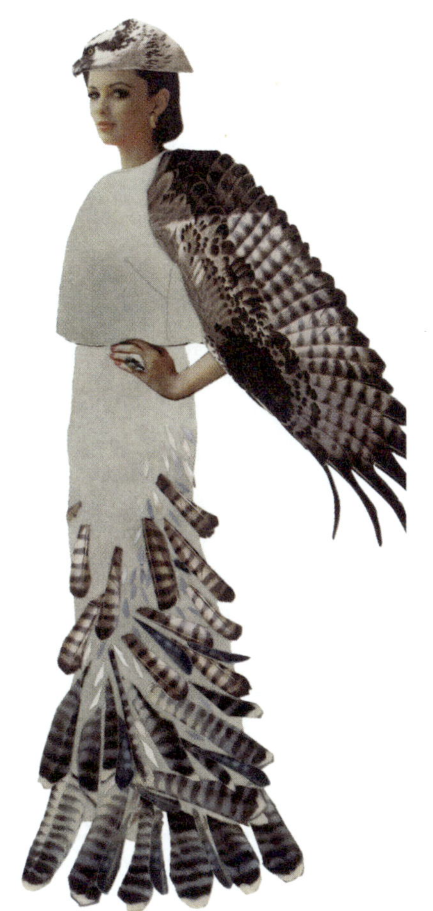

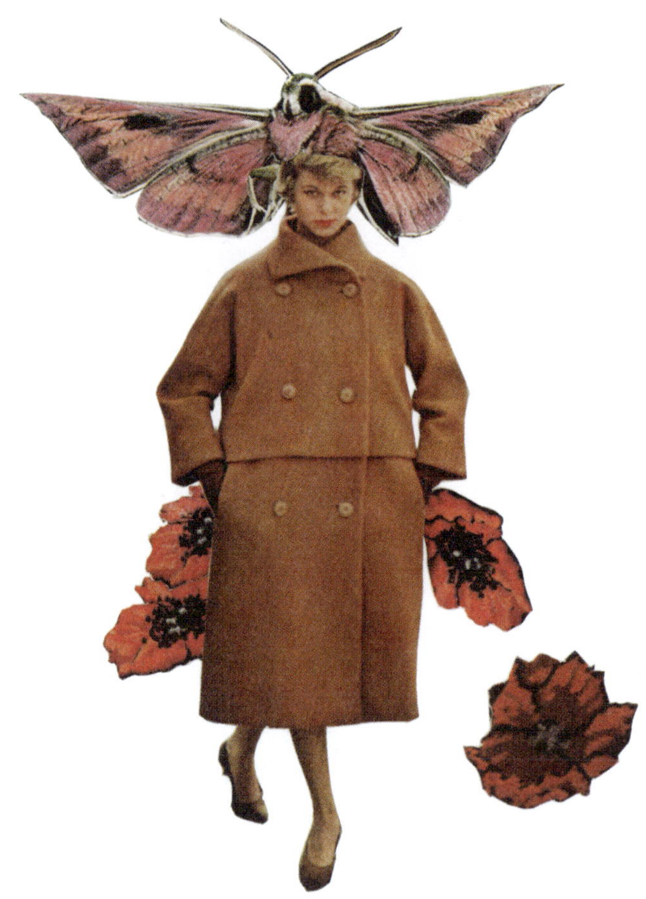

the only way out was to step to an edge and see —
to step out past an edge

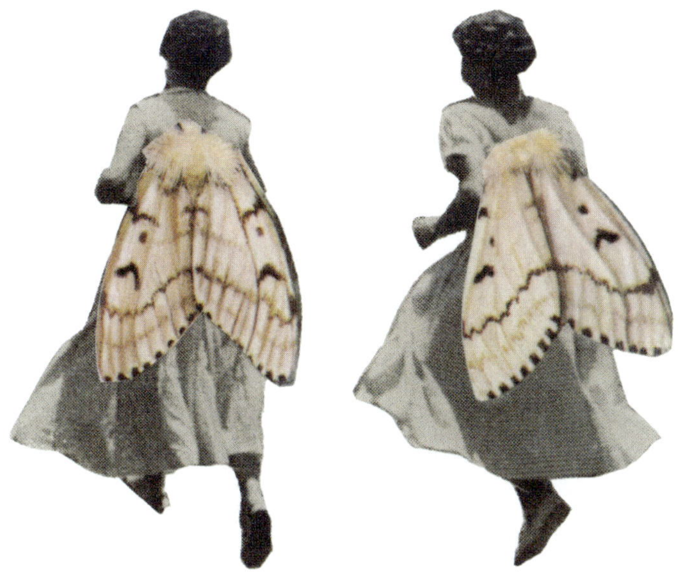

to angle my chin away,
veer off to —

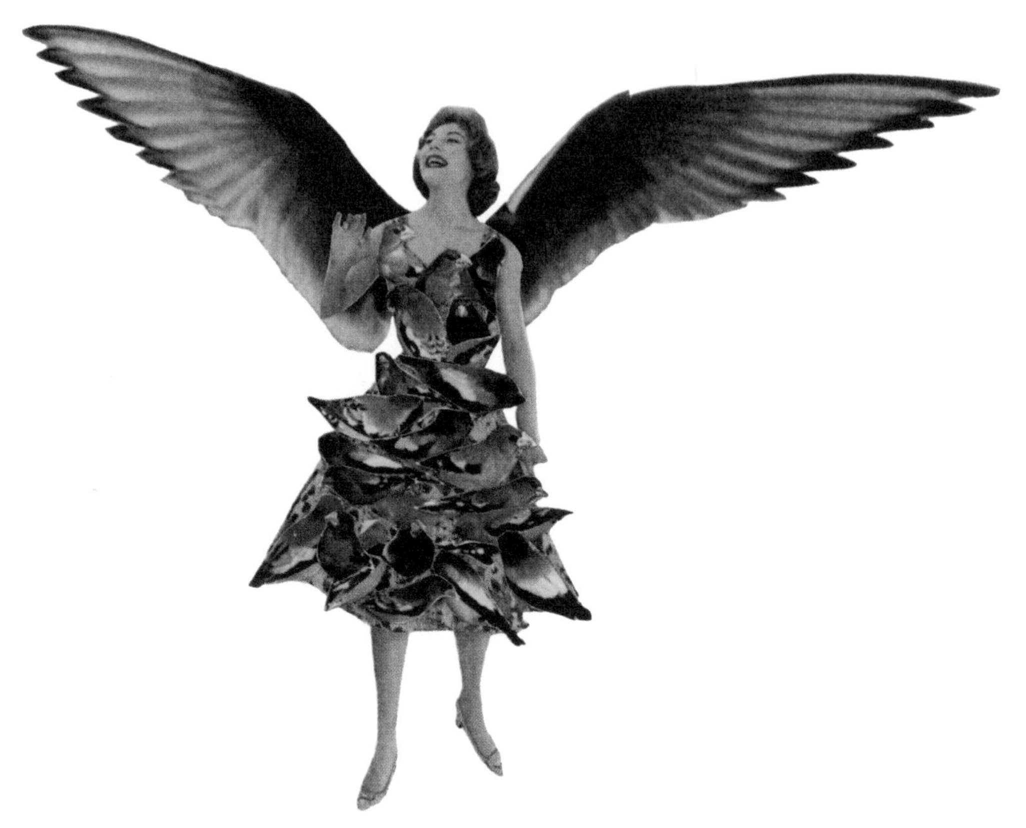

look — look —
another whole sky

Acknowledgements

Grateful acknowledgement to the editors of the following publications, where some of the poems and collages in this book first appeared, sometimes in different forms: the Academy of American Poets Poem-a-Day, *Bad Lineage, Barrow Street, Boston Review, Colorado Review, Diagram, Gettysburg Review, Hunger Mountain, The Georgia Review, Gulf Coast, New Ohio Review, New American Writing, On the Seawall, Oxidant Engine, Southeast Review,* and *Tupelo Quarterly.* A group of these poems won the Poetry Society of America's Alice Fay Di Castagnola award for a manuscript in progress, selected by Elisa Gabbert. Many of these poems and collages were made possible through the Saltonstall Residency (thank you Lesley Williamson), the Solarium Gallery (thank you Meghan Jordan), the framing skills of Stomping Grounds (thank you Bethany Haswell), and faculty research grants from Hobart and William Smith Colleges. I lifted the title "Looker" from a monotype by Nick Ruth. I lifted the pregnant spider from a poem by Tia Fishler. Alla Ivanchikova taught a class called "Monstrous Femininity" long before my art exhibition called "Feminine Monstrous," which contained many of the collages in this book. The cut-outs sequence was inspired by a beautiful conversation about woman-ing (and what to keep, and what to throw out) with Alice LeTowt. Thanks to these friends.

Geoff, Remi, Calder, Sobin, you are my dearest dears. Oh how I love you.

Full-hearted thanks to my parents, siblings, step-family, and in-laws, to those here and those gone, to my grandparents. Love and thanks to Donald Revell, who is family, and to Sue Wicklund, who is family. Michael Burkard, David Dick, Louise Glück, Grant Holly, Julie Paegle, Cadence Whittier: I miss you I miss you I miss you I miss you I miss you I miss you.

To my teachers, especially Karen Brennan, Kate Coles, Craig Dworkin, Susan Howe, Laurie Payne, Paisley Rekdal, Mike Rutter, and Kathryn Stockton, always and ever thank you. Shout out to HYFO and to all the astonishingly talented artists and writers I've been lucky enough to teach in 20-plus years at it, specifically to Aaron Eddy, Abbie Bloomheart, Abby Colvin, Rachel Faust,

Abbey Frederick, Alberto Garcia de la Puente, Alyssa Hamilton, Ana Schavoir, Andrew Merecicky, Andrew Pilet, Angelica Knudson, Annabel Ramsey, Beckett Hilton, Bevin O'Connor, Camille McGriff, Cecelia Ripley, Chelsey Blackman, Christina Roc, Claire Haudrich, Claire Kapitan, Clare McCormick, Claudia White, Cole Cassano, Cory Andrews, Emma Stratigos, Fiona Howes, Ergisa Xhuveli, Grace Snook, Haley Giunta, Hannah Bishop, Hannah Angelico, Hazel Brown, Holli Carrell, Irini Konstantinou, Jack Tafolla-Garcia, Jackson Bartell, Jens Olavson, Jill Crocetta, Kelly Craig, Lauren Chupp, Lito Weiss, Khaty Xiong, Khalym Burke-Thomas, Madeline Hanley, Matt Hogan, Maya Gunsberg, Meghan Moore, Megan Silverstein, Melissa Freitag, Meredith Groman, Nick Snow, Parker Condon, Saedra Blow, Sarah Kloos, Sarah Zeger, Tia Thevenin, Tim Carter, Willow Quine, Wren Andrews, Zoe Kusyk, and so many others.

Thank you to the amazing people at Fence, most especially the extraordinary and tireless Emily Wallis Hughes, who is right at Fence's beating heart, and also Shari DeGraw and Lydia Mead. To Heather Brown, once again, for everything, thank you. To my childcare providers, without whom the work would never happen, thank you—especially Izzy Boone.

Thank you to Elisa Gabbert, for buoying this book early on and to Kiki Petrosino for buoying it again later.

Thank you to my friends. Gosh I love you people. These dear ones helped specifically with this book, with drafts or paperwork or production or conversations about art or sheer timely friendship: Kazim Ali, Geoff Babbitt, Taylor Brorby, Julia Cilano, Melanie Conroy-Goldman, Chris Costello, Angela Daddabbo, Tia Fishler, Sue Gage, Robert Glick, Alice LeTowt, Elizabeth Libert, Rebecca Lindenberg, Jami Macarty, Kirin Makker, Cami Nelson, Max Piersol, Elim Pilet, Donald Revell, Anne Royston, Nick Ruth, Danny Schonning, Brenda Sieczkowski, Tina Smaldone, Beth Spencer, Laura Thérien, Claire Tranchino, Katelyn Weeks, David Weiss, and Elizabeth Willis.

There are ever more people to thank and love. These are some of my dearest friends, best colleagues, favorite writers, favorite people: Chris Abani, Albert Abonado, Kathleen Blackburn, Jeffrey Blankenship, Harmony Button, Lara Candland, Pete "PJ" Carlisle, Rob Carson, Marc Castro, Kim Castro, Jeff Chapman, Jenny Colville, Jackson Connor, Traci O Connor, Stephen Cope, Peter Covino, Anna Creadick, Shira Dentz, Danielle Deulen, Trista Emmer, Susan Goslee, Eryn Green, Natalie Green, Nathan Hauke, Jess Hayes-Conroy, Derek Henderson, Christina Houseworth, Brooke Johnson, Kirsten Jorgenson, Cáel Keegan, Claudia Keelan, Ingrid Keenan, Stacy Kidd, Matt Kirkpatrick, Esther Lee, Julie Lien, Joel Long, dawn lonsinger, Jason Magna, Christine Marshall, Rachel Marston, H May, Susan McCarty, James McCorkle, Joshua McKinney, Jennilyn Merten, Deb Moeller, Tim O'Keefe, Michael Palmer, Chris Patton, Jacob Paul Paul, Derek Pollard, Ben Ristow, Dan Rosenberg, Mary Ruefle, Wendy Scofield, Ely Shipley, Nicole Walker, Maggie Werner, Mike White, Marla Wick, Kira Witkin, Chris Woodworth, Rachel Yoder, Nissa Youngren, Burgi Zenhaeusern. Thank you, thank you—what luck to have found you all in this same world.

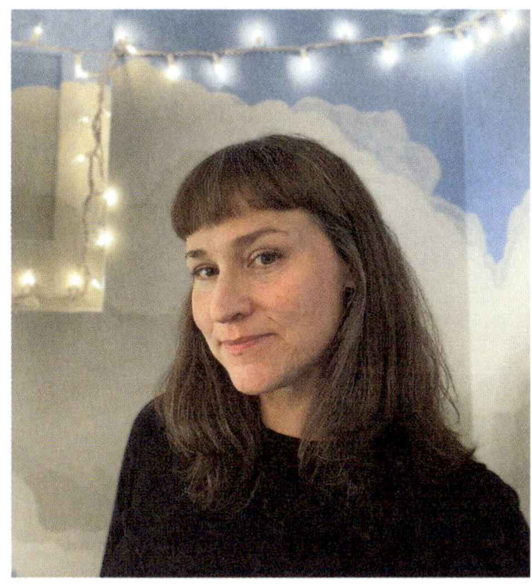

Kathryn Cowles's other books include *Maps and Transcripts of the Ordinary World* (Milkweed Editions) and *Eleanor, Eleanor, not your real name* (Bear Star Press), which won the Dorothy Brunsman Poetry Prize. Her poems and poem-photographs have been published in *Best American Experimental Writing, Boston Review, Colorado Review, Diagram, Free Verse, Georgia Review, Gulf Coast, New American Writing, Verse,* the Academy of American Poets Poem-A-Day, and elsewhere. She earned her doctorate from the University of Utah and is an associate professor of English at Hobart and William Smith Colleges in the Finger Lakes region of New York, where she directs (rotating) the Trias Residency for Writers and co-edits the Beyond Category section of *Seneca Review.*

Fence Books

FENCE MODERN POETS SERIES
Steven Alvarez *The Codex Mojaodicus*
Daniel Brenner *The Stupefying Flashbulbs*
Lee Ann Brown *In the Laurels, Caught*
Tess Brown-Lavoie *Lite Year*
Macgregor Card *Duties of an English Foreign Secretary*
Kathryn Cowles *The Strange Wondrous Works of Eleanor Eleanor*
Nick Demske *Nick Demske*
Donald Dunbar *Eyelid Lick*
Edgar Garcia *Skins of Columbus*
Kevin Holden *Solar*
Christopher Janke *Structure of the Embryonic Rat Brain*
Geraldine Kim *Povel*
Paul Legault *The Other Poems*
Jennifer Mackenzie *My Not-My Soldier*
Joyelle McSweeney *The Red Bird*
Kenneth Reveiz *MOPES*
Elizabeth Robinson *Apprehend*
Prageeta Sharma *The Opening Question*
James Shea *Star in the Eye*

THE OTTOLINE PRIZE
Amanda Deutch *new york ironweed*
Lesle Lewis *Rainy Days on the Farm*
Jennifer Nelson *On the Way to the Paintings of Forest Robberies*
Beth Roberts *Like You*
Kim Rosenfield *Phantom Captain*
Lauren Shufran *Inter Arma*
Stacy Szymaszek *Journal of Ugly Sites and Other Journals*
Wendy Xu *Phrasis*

FENCE MODERN PROSE SERIES
Mark Baumer, edited by Blake Butler and Shane Jones *The One on Earth*
Otessa Moshfegh *McGlue*
Hilary Plum *Strawberry Fields*
Valerie Werder *Thieves: A Novel*

Motherwell & Alberta Prize
Tina Brown Celona *The Real Moon of Poetry and Other Poems*
Rosemary Griggs *Sky Girl*
Harmony Holiday *Negro League Baseball*
Kasia Ullsvik Miller *Unspoiled Air*
Chelsey Minnis *Zirconia*
Ariana Reines *The Cow*
Sasha Steensen *A Magic Book*
Josie Sigler *living must bury*
Laura Sims *Practice, Restraint*
Elizabeth Marie Young *Aim Straight at the Fountain and Press Vaporize*

National Poetry Series
Simeon Berry *Ampersand Revisited*
Hannah Gamble *Your Invitation to a Modest Breakfast*
Kristin Hatch *the meatgirl whatever*
Douglas Kearney *The Black Automaton*
Jena Osman *The Network*
Ed Pavlić *Let's Let That Are Not Yet: Inferno*
Rodrigo Toscano *Collapsible Poetics Theater*
Laura Wetherington *A Map Predetermined and Chance*

Anthologies & Critical Works
Claudia Rankine, Beth Loffreda and Max King Cap, editors *The Racial Imaginary*
Walter Benjamin, translated by Carl Skoggard *The Sonnets*
Rebecca Wolff and Fence Editors, editors *A Best of Fence, The First Nine Years, Volumes I & II*
Catherine Wagner and Rebecca Wolff, editors *Not For Mothers Only: Contemporary Poets on
    Child-Getting & Child Rearing*

Poetry
Daniel Brenner *June*
Tina Brown *Celona Snip Snip*
Clark Coolidge *A Book Beginning What and Ending Away*
Clark Coolidge *88 Sonnets*
Martin Corless-Smith *Bitter Green*
Martin Corless-Smith *English Fragments A Brief History of the Soul*
Martin Corless-Smith *Swallows*
Michael Earl Craig *Can You Relax in My House*
Michael Earl Craig *Yes, Master*

FENCE BOOKS